fun • with
ponies
and horses

fun • with
ponies
and horses

HYLAS
PUBLISHING

HYLAS PUBLISHING

Publisher Sean Moore
Creative Director Karen Prince

First published by
Hylas Publishing
129 Main Street, Irvington,
New York 10533

Designed and produced by

studio **cactus** ltd

13 SOUTHGATE STREET   WINCHESTER   HAMPSHIRE   SO23 9DZ   UK
TEL 00 44 1962 878600 FAX 00 44 1962 859278
E-MAIL MAIL@STUDIOCACTUS.CO.UK   WEBSITE WWW.STUDIOCACTUS.CO.UK

Design Dawn Terrey, Laura Watson
Editorial Elizabeth Mallard-Shaw

First American Edition published in 2003

02 03 04 05 10 9 8 7 6 5 4 3 2 1

ISBN 1-59258-018-1

Printed and bound in England by Butler & Tanner Ltd
Color origination by Radstock Reproductions Ltd,
Midsomer Norton, UK

Distributed by St. Martin's Press

Contents

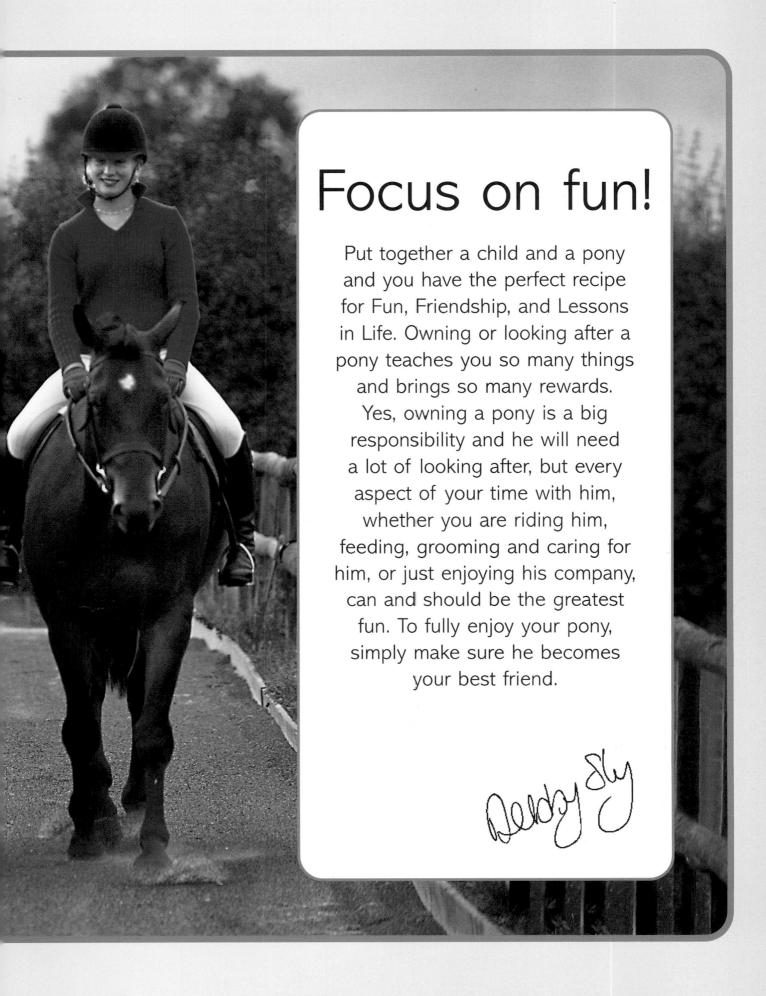

Focus on fun!

Put together a child and a pony and you have the perfect recipe for Fun, Friendship, and Lessons in Life. Owning or looking after a pony teaches you so many things and brings so many rewards. Yes, owning a pony is a big responsibility and he will need a lot of looking after, but every aspect of your time with him, whether you are riding him, feeding, grooming and caring for him, or just enjoying his company, can and should be the greatest fun. To fully enjoy your pony, simply make sure he becomes your best friend.

Debby Sly

You and your pony

Owning a pony is not just about having something to ride. Your pony needs looking after, and he also needs your friendship and attention. This is important not just for his health and well-being but for building a partnership with him, which is essential if you are both to get the best out of each other. Understand each other and you will enjoy each other.

Pony partners

The best way to get the most from your pony is to make him your friend. Think about your own life—it is your friends that you have the most fun with and your friends that you want to please and work with. So you should use the time you spend riding and caring for your pony in such a way that he wants to be your friend. By getting to know him well you will form a happy and confident partnership, and you will both enjoy yourselves.

Out and about

Shows and competitions are a good place to test and strengthen your partnership with your pony. Make sure he enjoys his day as much as you do. When you're ready for a burger and fries he's probably ready for some hay! While you enjoy an ice cream make sure he can have a drink of water. See Away days, pages 92–93.

Friends forever
Being friends isn't just about riding and competing. Take time to fuss over and befriend your pony when he's out in the field or in his stable. For one thing, if he is always pleased to see you he will always be easy to catch!

Back to school

Riding schools are a great way to get a taste of riding before you decide if you really want a pony. Choose one where they let you help with the grooming and tacking up so that you learn about caring for a pony as well as riding one. At school your favorite lessons are probably those taken by your favorite teacher, so when you choose a riding school make sure you like the person who is helping you—then you will improve.

Have an aim

You and your pony should have a goal to work toward. For some this may be to compete at the highest level, such as at the Kentucky Horse Trials. If you are not particularly competitive then simply aim to improve your riding skills to get the best out of your pony. Don't just drift aimlessly!

Join the club

The Pony Club is a worldwide youth organization for children who love ponies. It has rallies, competitions, tests, and pony camps, as well as information and activities for children who aren't lucky enough to own a pony. It is a great way to meet friends and learn at the same time. Some branches have links with local riding schools so that non-pony owners can "borrow" a pony.

Happy hacking

Riding out and about in the countryside is a great way to keep your pony fit and interested in life while you practise many of the things you have learned in lessons or read about. If you ride with a friend, you can help and encourage each other by watching each other practise new things.

Owning a pony

Your dream has come true and you can have your own pony. Now you must think long and hard about what would be the right pony for you. To enjoy a long and happy partnership, choose a pony who can not only do the things you want him to do but can also become your friend.

Ask a friend
Before taking on the responsibility of your own pony, why not stay for a few days with a friend who owns one? Join in with everything and get a better idea of what's involved.

It takes all sorts!
Horses and ponies come in many different shapes and sizes and, just like people, each one has a different personality. Your pony must suit your weight and size as well as your character. And it's important to remember that while you are still growing your pony will stay the same size—so choose carefully!

Off we go!

Choose a pony whose temperament and experience you can cope with. Like people, some ponies are very calm and relaxed in all but the most difficult circumstances, but they may lack energy and drive. Others may have plenty of get up and go but may also be unpredictable and difficult to control sometimes. For example, some ponies give little playful rears when they are over-excited and impatient to get going. Such horses can be great fun, but not if you are a nervous or highly strung type.

Mix and match

It's a good idea to try out several ponies before you buy one. That way you can begin to get a feeling for which sort of pony really suits you. Once you have found one that you think you might like, try riding him at all gaits and in different circumstances.

Buy a pony who shares the same ambitions as you—if you want to be a world champion while your pony just wants to enjoy being a cool dude, you'll find it difficult to get on!

Make sure you can sit comfortably on your pony. If he is too wide you won't be able to use your legs in the right place.

If your pony is too small it will be difficult for you both to keep your balance. Your pony may think that you should be carrying him!

Are you ready?

Owning a pony is a big commitment. Apart from the initial cost of buying the pony and finding somewhere for him to live, there's the expense of looking after him and buying all the equipment. Caring for a pony is a very responsible job, and takes up time every day of the week. To help you decide whether you really are prepared for it all, read through these questions and answer "yes" or "no" to each one.

1) Money matters

Have you got enough money to buy and care for your pony? You will need money for the following things:
- *Somewhere for him to live—either your own land and stables or at a livery yard (where you pay to have him kept)*
- *Food and hay*
- *Tack and equipment*
- *Shoeing*
- *Veterinary fees for regular health care, such as worming and dental checks, and extra fees if he becomes ill or injured*
- *Traveling to and competing in competitions*

2) Time to spare

Do you and your family have time to look after a pony? Even if he is not being ridden he must be checked every day to make sure he is not ill or injured. You will need:
- *Time to check him at least twice a day*
- *Time to feed and water him*
- *Time to groom and ride him regularly*
- *Time to maintain his field, stable, and all his equipment*

3) Shelter

Is there shelter and shade in your pony's field? Your pony will need some sort of shelter to protect him from the worst of the weather in winter and the heat and insects in summer. This can be:
- *High hedges and tall trees*
- *A field shelter (see right)*
- *A stable*

4) Helping hands

Who will help care for your pony if you are ill or away on holiday? You must either have someone who will look after him or be able to pay to send him to a livery yard. A helping hand will be needed:
- *If you go on holiday or a school trip*
- *If you are ill or injured*
- *If your parents are unable to take you to the place where your pony is kept*

5) Field duties

Do you have a paddock or field with safe, secure fencing and a good water supply? Every day someone must check that:
- *The fencing is still secure*
- *The water trough is full and clean*
- *The pony is safe and well*

6) Muck, muck, and more muck!

Are you prepared to get your hands dirty? You will get mucky:
- *Mucking out your pony's stable, shelter or paddock*
- *Washing and grooming your pony*
- *Cleaning his tack*

7) Pony pieces

Have you got all the kit you need to ride? Your pony will need:
- *A properly fitted saddle and bridle*
- *A saddle blanket (a pad that goes under the saddle)*
- *A headcollar*
- *A grooming kit*
- *Ideally, boots to protect his legs from injury*

8) All dressed up

Have you got the right clothing to ride safely? You will need:
- *A proper riding helmet or hat with safety harness*
- *Boots with a smooth sole and small heel so that your foot doesn't get trapped in the stirrup*
- *Ideally, riding jodhpurs or breeches—the seams on jeans will rub your skin*
- *Gloves*
- *A body protector if you want to go cross-country jumping, a proper riding jacket and competition jodhpurs if you want to compete*

9) Winter worries

When it's cold and wet will you be willing to go out and look after your pony? In the winter your pony may need you to:
- *Bring him into his stable*
- *Give him extra blankets either in his stable or out in the field*
- *Break the ice in his water trough each day so that he can drink*

10) His wardrobe

Are you able to buy the extra blankets and equipment your pony may need?

- *Blankets—either to wear in his stable or waterproof ones to wear in his field*
- *Boots and wraps for his tail and legs, to protect him when being ridden or travelling*
- *First-aid kit for minor cuts and injuries*

11) Going places

If you want to compete can you get transportation to competitions?
You will need:

- *A family member or friend who can drive*
- *A horse box or towing car and trailer…*
- *…or hire of a trailer or horsebox when needed*
- *Friends you can share transport with*

12) Dedication

Are you dedicated enough to look after your pony in all weathers every day?

- *If he is ill or injured and can't be ridden?*
- *Whether you win or lose at competitions?*

Mucking out

Mucking out has to be done every day so you must be sure that you are happy to do it. See what it's like by helping a friend who has a pony or ask at your riding school whether you can spend time caring for their ponies, as well as having riding lessons. That is a good way to find out what it is all like.

13) Fun, fun, fun

Do you want to have fun? A pony should be a source of tremendous fun and enjoyment. You can have fun:

- *Just being his friend*
- *Grooming and pampering him*
- *Riding him, alone or with friends*
- *Playing games and racing against your friends at home*
- *Competing at shows and events*
- *Learning to improve your skills together*

Decision time!

Once you have gone through all of the questions, look back at your answers. Think long and hard about any "no" answers—and then decide whether you are ready to own a pony. If you simply can't afford it, don't give up. You can still enjoy being with ponies by going to riding schools or sharing the care of a friend's pony. You will learn a great deal and, if you find out that owning a pony really is what you want, you will be well prepared for the day when you can have your own.

Knowing your pony

Get to know your pony by spending time watching and understanding his behaviour. Your pony cannot speak to you with his voice but his body language can tell you a great many things about how he is feeling. Learning to read his moods will help you to know whether he is happy or ill. You can also keep yourself out of harm's way by recognizing any warning signs that he is about to bite or kick out. Look and learn.

Follow my leader
When a horse follows behind his rider without being led, you know that a good relationship has been built up between him and his rider and he trusts her completely.

Horse talk
To encourage a pony to follow you, avoid eye contact while you make a fuss of him. Then turn your back or shoulder to him and walk quietly away. To get a pony to move away, you should make yourself as big as possible and stare him straight in the eye, in the same way as a wild stallion challenges any horse approaching him!

This healthy pony has well-toned muscles and is neither too fat nor too thin.

Grooming your pony daily keeps his coat in good condition—and helps you to get to know each other.

Once you are familiar with how your pony moves in all paces, you will be able to tell when there is discomfort in his legs or feet.

Funny or fighting

These ponies are playing, but horses sometimes forget how strong they are and end up hurting each other or a person. Always be aware of what all the ponies in the field are doing. Don't get caught up in their fun and games. If you think your pony is being bullied by the others, it is a good idea to move him to another field with a pony that will be kind to him.

Loopy lips!

A lower lip hanging loose shows that your pony is relaxed or resting. This pony's body language is indicating that he is both relaxed and alert—his lip is loose but his eyes and ears are definitely interested in something. He's probably thinking 'Here comes my rider, I'd better wake up!'

Your pony should be alert and interested in what's going on around him. Look for shiny, bright eyes.

Make sure that his nose is clean and dry.

Reading the signs

By watching your pony you will get used to what is 'normal behaviour' for him. Some ponies are always bright and alert, others are quiet and relaxed. You should be watching out for anything that is different from his normal behaviour or character. He may be cold, injured or worried about something. He will tell you if you look for the signs.

I'm all ears

Floppy ears mean that your pony is relaxed, perhaps even dozing. Ears pointing sharply forwards means his attention is on something ahead of him. When you are riding him, one ear flicking backwards and forwards means he is listening to you. Ears pinned flat back mean he is angry and may be about to bite or kick—so be careful!

What to wear

When it comes to what to wear when riding your pony, the only two really hard and fast rules apply to what you wear on your head and what you wear on your feet. Your riding hat is something that your life may depend upon, and you should never ride without a proper hat securely fastened with a safety harness. The basics that you will require in terms of clothing are shown here. But once you start competing you can keep adding to your wardrobe—there are different outfits for showing, hunting, cross-country riding, endurance riding and so on, as well as all sorts of accessories for each sport.

Slap on a hat
Riding hats or helmets have well-recognized standards. You should buy a hat that is made to the latest European or American standard, whichever is appropriate. If you have a fall and hit your head the hat should be replaced as it will have been weakened.

You usually wear cream-colored jodhpurs for competing, but dark colors are more practical for general riding.

Be safe, be seen
If you have to ride on the roads it is essential to make sure you are visible to other road users. It will be much easier for cars and trucks to spot you if you wear fluorescent kit. Dress yourself and your pony with reflective vest, armbands, and hat covers for you, and exercise sheets, leg and tail wraps for him. You can buy fluorescent strips to put on the bridle, and a special flashlight to go on your stirrup iron.

Feet first
Riding footwear should have a non-slip sole and a low heel to reduce the risk of your foot slipping through the stirrup iron—you would then be dragged by your pony if you fell off. Buy either short jodhpur boots or longer rubber or leather riding boots. Half-chaps can be worn with short boots to give your legs more protection.

Hey big spender!

Ponies and their equipment can soon start to cost a lot of money, so just buy the basics to start with. Secondhand riding wear is often available, especially through pony clubs and riding clubs (although it is always advisable to buy a new rather than used hat). Once you know which sports you are interested in, you can start to buy more specialist kit.

Body armor

Body protectors give you some protection in the event of a fall by padding your back, ribs, and shoulders. In most countries you have to wear one if you are going to do competitive cross-country riding. But it is worth wearing one whenever possible as you never know when you might fall off! You can buy them in bright colors and in many different styles.

Wear a loosely fitting sweatshirt or similar top that will allow full and free movement of your arms. You can buy showerproof types, which are especially practical.

Funny face

To brighten up your casual riding outfit you can buy different styles of helmet cover. The fun ones have all sorts of things on them—reindeer antlers, Santa Claus hats, animal faces, and pom-poms! Or you can buy multicolored and patterned covers like the ones the racing jockeys wear. If you are really fashion-conscious you can then buy the same color accessories for your pony, such as wraps, blankets, and saddle blankets.

Stretchy legs

Most jodhpurs and breeches are made from stretchy material to give you freedom of movement when riding. Jodhpurs have long legs and are designed to be worn with short boots; breeches, which finish below the knee, must be worn with long boots. You can buy them with "sticky bums," which help you feel more secure in the saddle!

Pampering your pony

You will probably spend more time caring for your pony than you will spend actually riding him, so it is important that you are happy to commit to this aspect of owning a pony. It should be fun and enjoyable for both of you, especially if you use your imagination to give him some special treats and to find new ways of pampering him.

Grooming

Grooming your pony is part of forming a partnership as well as a way of keeping him clean and healthy! In the wild, horses and ponies nibble and lick each other as part of a "getting to know you" process. They are really quite sociable, helpful animals and will stand nose to tail swishing the flies off each other. So get down to some grooming and make friends with your pony. Some days you will have time for only a quick brush over before you ride him, but on other days take the time to give him a full beauty treatment!

Bad hair day
Like people, some ponies always manage to look neat, tidy, and quite pretty. Others, well…

That tickles!

Some ponies love being groomed but others aren't so keen. This pony is trying to stop his friend nibbling his neck! Remember that if your pony has sensitive skin he may try to tell you that he has had enough. So watch for signs that he might be getting fed up—he may put his ears back or swish his tail.

You scratch my back…
Ponies groom each other partly to make and strengthen friendships and also for the practical reason that, despite their long legs, they cannot reach every part of their body that might itch. So it's a case of "You scratch my back, I'll scratch yours!"

Mud bath

During wet, cold weather your pony may roll around on the ground to cover himself in mud. He does this to keep warm. The mud insulates his coat and keeps the cold out and the heat in. If your pony has to live outside in cold weather, don't brush the mud off him unless you really have to. Brush the saddle, girth, and bridle areas only, so that his skin doesn't get rubbed when you ride him, and leave the rest of the mud to keep him warm.

Tidy tails

A full groom should include the tail. Use your fingers to tease out any twigs and other debris. Then you can use a body brush to start separating the hairs. Hard brushes can break the tail hairs.

Thanks, Mum

A mare reassures and comforts her foal by gently nuzzling him. She may also nibble the length of his mane. You can comfort your pony by copying this behavior—rubbing along the top of his neck with your hand.

Kit yourself out

Keeping your pony clean and tidy is easy if you have the right equipment. To start with, you really need only one or two brushes and combs, and a hoofpick, but to get the perfect look you can buy all sorts of bits and pieces to help make your pony beautiful. Write your pony's name on all his personal equipment and use it just for him. Just as you like to have your own toothbrush, it's healthier for your pony to have his own kit.

Kit bag
Keep all your pony's grooming kit on an easy to carry box. Then you can pick it all up together and take it with you, whether you are going to your pony's field, stable or off to a show.

Dandy brush
This is quite a stiff brush, which is used to brush off the worst of the dust and mud from the body and neck. It is usually too hard and scratchy to use on a pony's face or in very tickly areas.

Tail comb
This is meant to be used to comb through your pony's tail, but you will usually find the hair is too tangled. Use a body brush to brush off any mud, then shake out any bedding or bits of grass. Use the tail comb only after you have brushed, washed, and conditioned the tail to get the tangles out—otherwise you may end up with a bald, very sore pony.

Body brush
This is a softer, gentler brush than the dandy brush and can be used on your pony's face and around any other sensitive areas. It will lift the dust and grease out of your pony's coat, so use it after you have used the dandy brush on the main parts of his body. The body brush can also be used on your pony's mane and tail.

Grooming or massaging mit *If you wear this rubbery creation on your hand like a glove you'll find it's easy to groom or massage those awkward knobbly bits of your pony's body, such as his knees, hocks, and hip bones.*

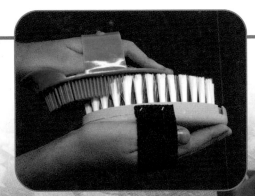

Plastic curry-comb

The plastic curry-comb is used to scrape the dirt and dust out of the grooming brushes. It can also be used to remove thick mud from your pony's coat.

Sponges

Use a damp sponge to wipe your pony's ears, eyes, nose, and mouth. Use a separate one for cleaning the sheath and under the dock. Keep different-color sponges for each job.

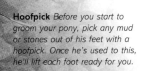

Hoofpick *Before you start to groom your pony, pick any mud or stones out of his feet with a hoofpick. Once he's used to this, he'll lift each foot ready for you.*

Mane comb

This is used to smooth and detangle your pony's mane. If there's a lot of mud in his mane you can use the plastic curry-comb to brush it out, then use this comb for finishing touches. If the mane is very tangled, it is better to wash it and use a conditioner, as you would your own hair, rather than risk pulling all the hair out by tugging with a comb. It can also be used to 'pull' your pony's mane (*see page 31*).

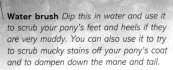

Water brush *Dip this in water and use it to scrub your pony's feet and heels if they are very muddy. You can also use it to try to scrub mucky stains off your pony's coat and to dampen down the mane and tail.*

Polished off

Use a dampened cloth or a soft sheepskin mit to give your pony's coat a final polish. You can buy all sorts of conditioning sprays that will make your pony's coat extra specially glossy and you can rub these on with the cloth or mit. But do remember that all the polishing in the world will not make your pony's coat shine if he is not well. If he has a dull coat, make sure there is nothing wrong with him rather than try to cover it up.

Just for fun

We all enjoy getting dressed up or being pampered as a special treat, and there are all sorts of things you can do to your pony to make him feel extra special and beautiful, too. If you are competing at a show, your pony is expected to be turned out in a neat, traditional manner (*see* pages 96–97). But when you're just chilling out at home you can be far more imaginative and turn your pony into a supermodel!

Using ribbons
You can have lots of fun with ribbons. If you're skilled at braiding, braid them into your pony's tail or mane. Or you can tie the ribbons in bows. Either way, try using several colors together.

Trimming a tail

Make sure your pony's tail is clean and well brushed before you get ready to trim it. Then decide exactly what length you want the tail to end up (see right). When you are ready, stand slightly to the side of your pony, rather than directly behind him, so that he can see what you are doing. Run your hand down his tail and hold all the hair together in one bunch a little way from the end. With a fairly good-size pair of sharp scissors, cut neatly across the tail to trim off the ends. Try to keep the cut straight. You can always trim any stray bits off separately.

How short?
Most tails look good when they finish a few inches (centimeters) below the point of the hock. Some ponies carry their tail higher when they are moving than when they are standing, so don't cut too much off at first. Watch him move before deciding to trim more. Never trim the tail above hock level.

Browbands

Brighten up your pony's browband by decorating it with a velvet ribbon—or two ribbons—in your favorite color. Take the browband off the bridle to do this as it's a bit tricky.

Start at one end of the browband and leave a short tail of ribbon sticking out. Secure it in place by wrapping the rest of the ribbon tightly round on itself a couple of times.

Carefully wind the ribbons round the browband, working along its full length, holding the ribbons taut and overlapping a bit each time so that the browband is completely covered.

When you get to the other end of the browband tuck the spare end of ribbon back through the last twist and cut it off so that it's the same length as the little tail you left at the other end.

Bows in the mane

When you use ribbons on your pony's tail, use a matching color to decorate the mane too. Braid the ribbon into the mane or tie bows round sections along the top of the mane or at the end of the braids.

Fancy feet

You can shine up your pony's hooves with hoof oil or ointment, but if you want him to be really eyecatching try some glitter or sequins. You can buy them ready made or you can simply stick sequins or glitter on while the ordinary hoof oil or ointment is still wet. Never use glue!

Quarter marks

In photographs or at shows, you may have seen horses and ponies with all sorts of patterns brushed onto their hindquarters. These are called quarter marks. If you want to give a serious impression you should stick to geometric shapes, such as squares and diamonds. You can buy ready-made stencil sheets for these. But if you are a little more artistic, you can have fun making your own stencils or designing your own comb patterns.

Stencil patterns

First things first

Stencil and comb patterns show up very clearly on a sleek and shiny summer coat. So before you try out your design, start by grooming your pony really well, and get rid of any dust and grease by giving his coat a wipe over with some coat shine or baby oil.

Tricky bits

With some designs, you might find it easier to use a comb rather than a brush to put the pattern on. A comb makes it easier to get right into the corners and edges of the stencil so the pattern comes out sharper.

Making a stencil

You can use ready-made stencils to make patterns ("quarter marks") on your pony's hindquarters, but it is much more fun to make your own, original patterns.

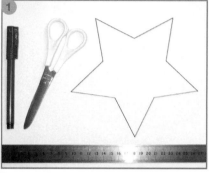

Draw your design on a sheet of thick paper or card, then cut it out, leaving a hole in the card. Choose a bold, simple design, such as a star, a heart, or the first letter of your name.

With a soft, damp brush, smooth down the hair on your pony's rump or shoulder. Hold the stencil in position and brush gently over the pattern, in the opposite direction to the way the hair grows.

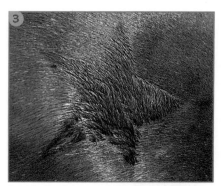

Carefully lift off the stencil. Now your pony has his own designer coat! This works better in summer, when your pony's coat is short and shiny, than in winter, when it is thick and fluffy.

Comb patterns

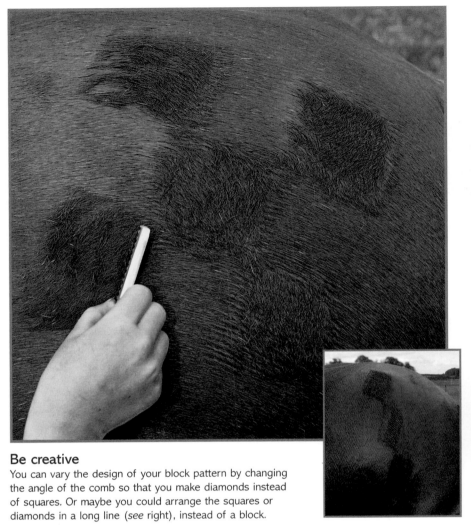

An easy pattern to make using a comb is a block of squares, like a section of a chessboard. The hair in one square goes in a different direction from that in the square next to it.

First smooth down your pony's coat with a soft, damp sponge or body brush. Then, with a small mane comb, working in the opposite direction to the way the hair grows, make a small square on his hindquarters.

Next to it, leave a square of the same size combed the way the hair grows. Next to that, comb another square in the opposite direction. Keep the squares evenly spaced and in line to make a chessboard.

Be creative
You can vary the design of your block pattern by changing the angle of the comb so that you make diamonds instead of squares. Or maybe you could arrange the squares or diamonds in a long line (*see* right), instead of a block.

Pattern ideas

Clover leaf

Batman

Words and letters

Pulling tail and mane

Your pony's mane and tail can either be left naturally long and shaggy or you can pull them, which means thinning and shortening them. Pulled manes are easier to comb. However, pulling is done primarily for appearance, and is not very comfortable for the pony, so if he has to live at grass a lot it is kinder to leave his mane and tail long. Remember that if you pull his tail it is then not possible to braid it, and you will need to keep pulling it regularly to keep it neat.

Pulling power
Pulled manes and tails keep your pony looking tidy, especially when competing.

Pulling the tail

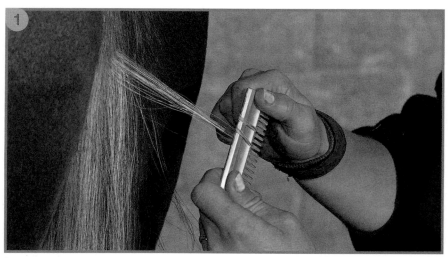

Start at the top, on one side of the tail and take a few hairs from the underside of the dock (the bony bit). Wrap these round a comb and, with a quick tug, pull them out.

Safety tip

Be aware that your pony might object to having his tail hairs pulled out. It helps if you do not try to pull out too many hairs at once. (As with your own head, pulling a couple of hairs is a lot less painful than pulling a handful!) If you are not sure about how your pony will react, ask an adult to do it the first time. You can stand a bale of hay, straw, or bedding between the pony's hind leg and the person pulling the tail, which will give some protection if the pony should suddenly kick out.

Work your way down both sides of the dock, pulling out hair, little by little from the underside of the tail. The tail will end up smooth and narrow at the top, but full and flowing at the bottom

Pulling the mane

Pulling the mane will shorten it and thin it at the same time. Comb through the mane to make sure there are no tangles. If the mane is full of knots the pulling process will be more uncomfortable for the pony.

Hold a few strands of mane and back-comb the rest of the hair out of the way. To thin the mane back-comb right to the top and pull the strands out completely. To shorten it back-comb to the length you want it to be.

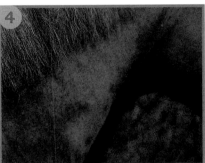

Wrap the few strands of hair around the comb so that they cannot slip out and with a short sharp tug, pull the hairs out. Then stand back to check that the result is neat and tidy (4).

Happy and hairy
Mountain and Moorland breeds usually have their manes and tails left in their natural state—that is, long and shaggy. The feathers and hairs are usually left on the legs as well.

A tail wrap will smooth down the tail and protect it from rubbing if you travel your pony in a horsebox or trailer. The wrap should be firm enough not to slip, but not tight.

Lift the pony's tail and start by putting the wrap under his tail, as high as you can get it. Keep hold of the free end, wind the wrap round once, then tuck the free end in and wind the wrap over it.

Keep winding the wrap round and round the tail, gradually working your way down from the top to the end of the dock. Make sure you overlap the wrap by half to a third each time.

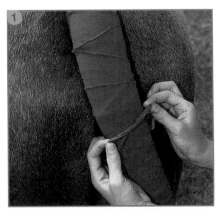

Work your way back up the tail until the wrap runs out. Tie a loose but neat bow with the wrap strings. You can then tuck the bow under one layer of wrap to cover it up.

Braiding mane and tail

Braiding a pony's mane and tail is the traditional way to turn him out for occasions such as shows and hunting. If your pony's tail is pulled, you can not braid it, but you should still braid his mane. Braiding the tail takes a bit more practise but the result is very impressive if you get it right! Remember that some pony breeds should be shown with mane and tail in their natural, loose state, so before braiding for a show check the turnout rules for your pony type. Whether or not you braid, your pony's coat, mane, and tail should be clean and tidy.

Braiding mane

1 It is easier to braid a short, pulled mane (*see* pages 30–31) than it is to braid a thick shaggy one. Before you start, take a damp body brush and smooth the mane down flat.

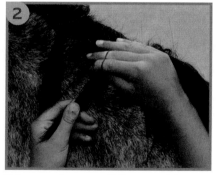

2 Using your fingers, split the mane into bunches of even size. Remember that the bigger the bunch, the bigger and fatter each braid will be. Secure each bunch with an elastic band.

3 Take one bunch. Remove the elastic band and split it into three even sections ready for braiding. (You can use a special three-pronged comb-like tool to do this or you can just do it with your fingers.)

4 Braid each bunch as tightly as you can. Take the left-hand section and cross it over the middle section; then take the right-hand section and cross it over the middle section.

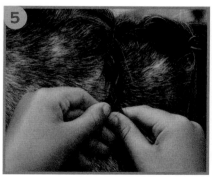

5 Continue in this way, keeping the braid really tight, until you have worked as far down the bunch as you can. When you get to the end, secure it with an elastic band, wrapping the band around several times.

6 Fold the braid up underneath itself once or twice to form a neat little ball tight against your pony's neck. Secure it in position with another elastic band. Braid your pony's forelock in the same way.

Braiding tail

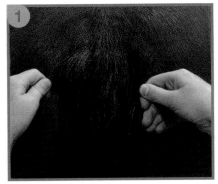

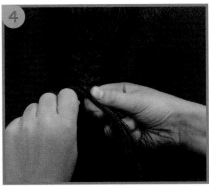

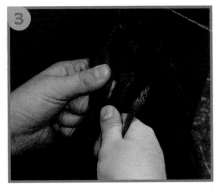

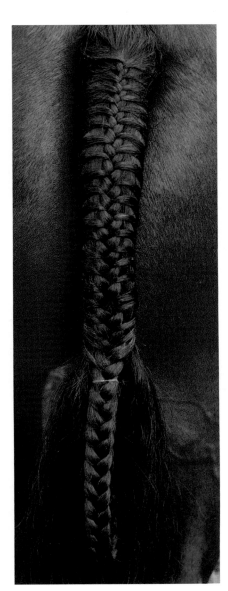

To braid the tail take two sections of hair from the top of the tail, one from each side of the tail. Take a third section (which will form the middle section) from the middle of the tail. Make sure each section of hair is the same thickness.

Pass the left section of tail over the middle section, then the right section over the middle. At this point take another section from the left of the tail, and pass this over the middle; then do the same for the right. Keep each new section the same size.

Continue in this way, taking new sections of hair from each side of the tail and braiding them in with the section of hair from the middle of the tail. You will also need to keep picking up more hair from the middle as you work your way down.

The secret to creating a good tail braid is to pull the pieces gathered in from the side of the tail as tight as you can. And make sure the middle of the braid is in the middle of the tail.

Once you get to the end of the dock, stop taking hair from the sides and just braid the three sections of hair you are left with into one long thin braid. Secure the end with an elastic band.

Now fold the long thin braid back on itself so that the end of it is tucked in behind the point where it starts. Secure it in place with another elastic band. Use a tail wrap or tail guard to cover and protect the braid. Remove it carefully!

Manes

Different ponies have differently shaped necks. Some are short and chunky, while others are long and elegant. Experiment and make braids of different sizes to see which suits your pony best. Usually bigger, chunkier braids look best on thick, chunky necks, and small, neat braids look best on long, elegant necks. To make a really neat and effective-looking forelock braid, start if off in the same way as you braid the tail. Then, as you get to the longer hairs, you simply continue with a normal braid.

Running braid

Start by braiding a small bunch of hair at the top end of your pony's neck. Use quite a thin bunch of mane so you form a narrow braid. Now braid to about two-thirds of the way down the bunch.

Now bring in a small section of hair from the rest of your pony's mane and braid it into the first braid. Hold the original braid tightly with one hand while you bring the new piece of mane into it with the other.

Keep taking another small section of mane and braid it in to the original braid, trying to guide the shape of the braid in a nice line along the neck. Pull each new piece quite tight to help you form a good line.

Running short

The running braid may get to a point where the sections of mane you want to bring in to it aren't long enough to reach the main braid. Secure the original braid with an elastic band and then start the process again from the opposite end of your pony's mane.

Beautifully braided

A running braid like the one shown suits ponies with long fine manes. It is a quick and easy way of turning out a pony in a neat, original way. Leave the forelock unbraided when you do this type of braid.

Crochet braiding

Divide your pony's mane up into evenly sized bunches, and secure each one with a rubber band. The bunches can be thicker than for normal braids as they are going to be divided up again and again.

Split two adjoining bunches into two and then bring the left-hand section of one across to meet the right-hand section of the other. Split the bunch carefully so you don't end up with straggly hairs hanging loose.

Secure both sections together using an elastic band, making sure they join in the middle of the two original bunches to form a diamond shape. Adjust each elastic band to keep all the "diamonds" the same size.

Keep splitting each bunch and joining half of one to half of the other in the same way until you produced a crochet or net effect.

Hairy Hair Net

This type of braid works well on a pony with a long thick mane. You can braid the forelock normally to finish off this striking hairstyle!

Bathtime

On a warm sunny day, when you have time on your hands, give your pony a spring clean from top to toe. Not only will he look better for it, but it will get rid of all the loose hairs, dirt, and grease that clog up his skin. Use buckets of warm water if you can as the heat will help lift the grease and dirt more easily. Cold water might be quite a shock to your pony, especially if he has been standing in the warm sun!

Hosing down

Spraying your pony with a garden hose is a quick way of rinsing off shampoo once you have finished washing him, but he may take a while to get used to the spray from the hose. It is also a quick and easy way to cool him down in hot, sunny weather.

17 Equipment head

A. *Sweat-scraper* **B.** *Bucket* **C.** *Towels*
D. *Shampoo* **E.** *Sponge*

Washing the tail
Dunk your pony's tail into a bucket of warm soapy water and work the shampoo into the hair. Rinse very thoroughly with clean water. Swish the tail around to dry it off.

Hair wash

Wet the mane, then pour some shampoo into your hands and rub it in well, right down into the roots. To avoid getting shampoo in your pony's eyes, lift his forelock back between his ears and wash it as part of his mane.

Scrape away

Once you have washed and rinsed your pony, use a sweat-scraper to squeeze all the excess water out of his coat. Scrape it firmly, but without knocking or banging his bony bits, and work in long sweeping strokes, going in the same direction that his hair grows.

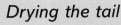

Drying the tail

Standing to one side, take hold of your pony's tail just below the dock. Then swirl his tail round and round like a propeller to help it dry. Now use a detangler spray, your fingers, and a comb, to get all the knots out.

Towel dry

As a final treat, use some towels to massage and dry him off. You must work gently around his face and ears but you can rub quite hard around the main parts of his neck and body.

3

Fun and games

There are so many things you can do to enjoy your pony and make the most of your time together. And the best of fun is usually had when you join up with friends and their ponies and take part in activities or games together. Choose the things you really enjoy doing, and have fun while you all learn from each other. Your pony will have a good time too!

Pony parties

Spending time with a pony is a great way to make new friends, and the more friends you have the more fun you can have. You don't have to go to shows and competitions; you can have fun at home by racing and competing against your friends and organizing all sorts of games. Picnics, fun rides, camps, and rallies are all part of the fun you can have with other pony-mad people. You can all help each other.

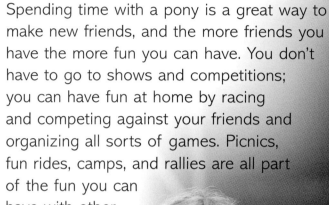

Learning together
Group lessons are a good way of learning together. They give you all a chance to watch each other, which will help you to gain confidence and improve your own riding. Then you can practise all that you have learnt together at home. Don't be afraid to ask each other for help or ideas.

Change the scene
Get together with friends at different locations to ride and practise with each other. It's good for your pony to learn to settle and concentrate in different atmospheres. So have everyone round to your place one day, and then all go to a friend's house next time.

★ *It's good to talk*

Make friends and learn lots of horse and pony facts by logging onto the Internet (with an adult's permission). There are lots of horsey sites where you can swap notes and photographs with like-minded pony pals. Some sites have sections where you can put questions to equestrian experts.

Enjoy yourself!

Riding and owning a pony should, first and foremost, be good fun. Do the things you enjoy and take time just to relax and make the most of the friendship of both your four-legged and two-legged friends.

Happy camping

If you join a local branch of the Pony Club you may get the chance to go on a Pony Club camp. Everyone takes a pony and enjoys organized lessons, riding competitions, quizzes, and all sorts of activities. You can also train for some of the Pony Club tests.

Working together

Taking good care of your pony's health and welfare is essential to good horsemanship, and at Pony Club camp you can have fun—and learn a lot—from sharing stable chores. Here, temporary stables enable all the ponies to live next door to each other.

Relays and races

Obstacle racing games are a great way to have fun and learn new skills at the same time. The games are similar to the ones played over 100 years ago by soldiers in India; they were called *gymkhana*, which meant gymnastic displays on horseback. You can enter gymkhanas at local shows—and win prizes if you're fast enough—but you can also play at home with your friends.

Practise bending in walk or trot. Then try it in canter, as this pony is doing

What's all the noise?

To be good at gymkhana games you need to teach your pony not to be afraid of the equipment or the noise that some of the games make. So, before you start, quietly let your pony look at and smell

the equipment, talking to him all the time to reassure him. Ride him around the blocks and bales or poles until he is happy to go right up close to them. Get a friend to drop potatoes into a bucket so that he gets used to the noise this makes. If your pony is confident about what he is doing then you have more chance of winning!

Bending race

For this, you ride from the start line to a row of blocks, such as large buckets or bales of straw. (Poles or stakes should not be used as they can be very dangerous.) Weave in and out of the blocks, and when you get to the end race to the finish line. This race is extremely good for developing the effective use of your legs and improving hand and leg coordination.

Musical chairs

For this game you need several chairs or blocks and someone to be in charge of the music. Start with one chair fewer than the total number of players. Ride round the chairs until the music stops; then jump off and sit down. Whoever is left without a chair is out. Then remove one chair and continue the game until only the winner is left. It's great practise for getting on and off!

Egg-and-spoon race

In this game you race from the start to the finish line while balancing an egg on a spoon. (Use hard-boiled eggs for this, not raw ones!) If you drop the egg you have to get off, pick it up, and get back on again. Try it in walk first before trotting or cantering. It will improve your balance and teach you to keep your hands still.

Neck-reining

Neck-reining is a term used to describe steering your pony. To turn your pony to the right, move your body slightly to the right and move your hand so the rein is pressed against the left side of his neck. Do the opposite to turn left.

Most gymkhana games involve quick changes of direction and speed, steering with one hand, and occasionally leaning out of the saddle, teaching you good balance. This is an essential part of riding well.

Use your legs to help steer the pony.

What a racquet!

You can use a tennis racquet and ball instead of an egg and spoon. In either case the secret is to keep your hands still even though your pony is moving. This improves your riding because good riding requires steady hands. Every time your hands move your pony can feel this on his mouth, so the steadier your hands are the more comfortable your pony will be.

Stepping stones
For this game you use a line of bales as stepping stones. Race up to the bales and jump off your pony. Leading him beside you, step across from bale to bale as fast as you can. Jump back on and race to the finish line.

Sock race

Persuade some friends to stand at the finish line, each holding out several pairs of socks. Each rider races up to a person, grabs a pair of socks, races back, and drops them in a bucket. Then the riders race back for the next pair and so on. The winner is the first rider to get all their socks in the bucket.

Walk, trot, canter race

This race is good for helping you to control your pony's paces. All line up at the start and walk as fast as you can to the finish line. Turn round and trot back to the start, turn again and race back to the finish in canter. If your pony trots when he should be walking, or canters instead of trotting, you have to turn a circle before continuing in the correct pace.

Vaulting race

Vaulting onto your pony is the quickest way of getting on in a race, but it takes practise. Run beside your pony's shoulder while resting your left hand on his withers. Reach over his back with your right hand and hold the saddle. Spring upwards and forwards and swing your right leg over your pony's back. To begin with try doing it from a standstill, and then let someone lead him while you practise it at a run.

Horseball relay

This is a team relay race. Stand half your team behind the finish line and the other half behind the start line. The first rider races from start to finish carrying a horseball. As he crosses the line he passes it to the next rider, who then races back and passes it to the next team member, and so on. Before you start, make sure all the ponies are familiar with the horseball and are not frightened of it.

No cheating!

Use showjump poles as the start and finish lines so that there can be no cheating. Everyone has to start behind the poles and finish by crossing right over them. Poles are also a lot safer than tape, which can become tangled up with everything.

Having a ball

If you enjoy the rough and tumble of team sports then ball games on horseback are something that you and your pony could enjoy together. Polo, polocrosse, and horseball are all team ball games that provide fast and furious action—once you've had a bit of practise! Most pony clubs offer a good introduction to one or all of these sports, and there are a growing number of clubs that run both junior and senior leagues. Polocrosse and horseball are particularly popular as they require less horse-power and expense than the glamorous world of polo demands. Many ponies adapt brilliantly to these games once they get used to what their rider is trying to do!

Polocrosse

Three players (from a team of six) play alternate "chukkas" (periods of play lasting 8 minutes). Each game has six chukkas and is played on a rugby-size pitch. The ball is thrown and caught with a long racquet with a net on the end of it. A goal is scored by throwing the ball between two goalposts set 8ft (2.5m) apart.

Horseball

This game is played on a small grass pitch (75 × 32yd/70 × 30m) with two teams of four players. A football fitted with six leather handles is thrown from player to player, with opposing team players trying to intercept it. A goal is scored by shooting it through a hoop at the end of the pitch. If the ball is dropped the player must scoop it up off the ground by stretching down from his pony.

Polo

To play polo you need two ponies as this fast-action game is too exhausting for one! The pitch is large, 300 × 200yd (274 × 183m), with a goal at each end. The game is played by two teams of four players. Each player has a long-handled mallet made of cane, which is used to control a hard ball. As in hockey, each player is marked by a member of the opposing team, who tries to gain control of the ball and hit it into the opponent's goal. Each game consists of six rounds, called chukkas, each lasting 7½ minutes.

DIY ball games

Horseball and polocrosse can easily be practised at home with friends. (Polo is more difficult because it requires each player to have more than one pony.) Go with a group of friends to a club to learn the basics and to introduce your pony properly to the game. Then practise at home together. You can have a horseball made by asking a saddler to sew six straps onto a leather football to make handles.

Get protected

For all these games you need to wrap your pony's legs put on or boots to protect him from being knocked by sticks, balls, or other ponies. They will also provide some support, which is important as he will be doing far more twisting and turning and stopping and starting than is required in most other sports. (For all these games, your pony must be very fit and agile.) His tail should also be fully wrapped so that it cannot become caught up in other riders' equipment. This polo player has sensibly protected himself as well by wearing knee pads. Face guards can also be worn.

Costume parties

Costume parties on horseback can be great fun, especially if you can think of a theme that is related to horses, such as knights in armor, the Wild West, warrior princesses, and so on. With a little imagination you could come up with something a bit different, such as using a bamboo pole and some old clothes to make yourself into a "clothes horse!" There are any number of similar ideas, but make sure it is obvious what you are supposed to be! You can rent or borrow a costume, but it is more fun to make your own.

Dress your pony too!

Don't leave your pony out of the fun; decorate his tack and/or his tail and mane in keeping with your costume.

Medieval costumes

Medieval costumes are quite easy to make. These ones have been created from old clothes and simple materials, and they did not take very long to put together. You can have a go at making them yourself by following the instructions on pages 54–55.

Dress sense

Whatever costume you choose, always put on a riding hat once you are ready to get in the saddle Then make sure it's all comfortable and you can still hold the reins and control your pony. Try it all on before the event so your pony gets used to it.

Princess

Clown

Raj

Dutch maid

Hawaiian babe

Pierrot

A knight to remember

It is really easy to make your own super knight's costume. All you need to make fantastic chain mail is some bubble wrap (it looks just like the real thing when you spray it silver). The costume shown here is a crusader's uniform with a bright red cross, but you can choose a different emblem if you like. By adding a crown you can make yourself king for the day. Invite your friends round and make up your own tournament games (see p.36).

(see p.36)

Dress your pony, too!
Don't leave your pony out of the fun. He'll make a wonderful knight's steed if you decorate his blanket with bunting. Strips of crêpe paper in a color to match your emblem and cut into triangles are ideal for this.

17 Equipment head

A. Plastic bottle **B.** Silver spray **C.** Duck tape **D.** Bubble-wrap **E.** Silver felt **F.** Paper **G.** Red felt **H.** Scissors **I.** Pencil

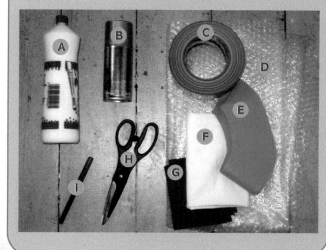

Making the tunic

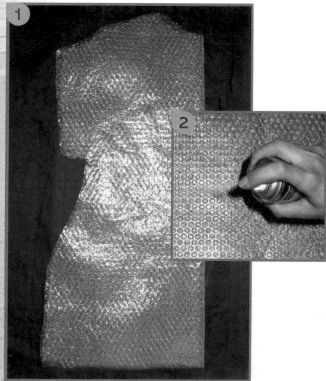

Lay a large T-shirt on a sheet of bubble-wrap, draw round it, then cut out the tunic shape. Fold the tunic lengthways to check the shape is even on both sides **(1)**. Spray the bubbly side silver **(2)**. Repeat for the back.

Draw your crusader's insignia on to a piece of paper or card **(3)** and cut it out to create a template. A simple cross is all you need for the front but you can put something more exciting on the back: a dragon, a snake, or bolt of lightning. Next, simply trace around your template on to a piece of colored felt **(4)**. Finally, cut out your emblem and glue it on to a square of white cloth.

Hats on!

Remember that unless you are being led by an adult, you will have to wear a riding hat under your costume party headgear. You can cut out a knight's helmet from silver cardboard, designing it to wrap round your hat.

Make a collar for your tunic **(5)**. Fold a circle of grey felt in half and then cut out a semicircle that matches the size of the tunic's neck. If the collar is too small to go over your head, cut small slits halfway into the collar so that it will open slightly as you put it on.

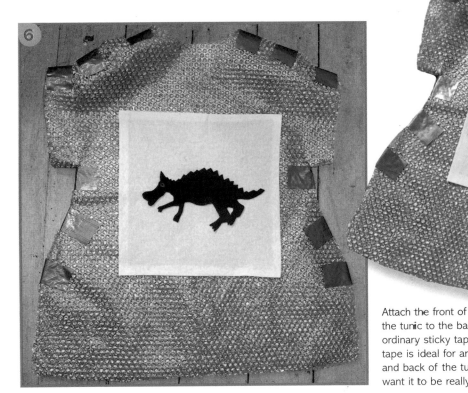

Attach the front of the tunic to the back using tape— ordinary sticky tape will do, but silver duck tape is ideal for armor. Finally, glue your emblem on to the front and back of the tunic **(6)**, or ask an adult to stitch it on if you want it to be really strong.

Ribbons and rosettes

If you enter competitions it probably won't be all that long before you are winning prizes and starting a collection of rosettes to stick on your pinboard. But even if you don't go into competitions (or you haven't managed to win any prizes yet), you can have lots of fun making your own rosettes at home. And the big bonus here is that you can choose your own colour scheme (so you can always win the first prize!). Or, if you enjoy decorating your pony's browband (see page 27), you could use the same ribbon to make him—and yourself—a matching rosette.

Mix and match

The rosette on the opposite page has been made using red, white, and blue ribbons and crêpe paper but obviously you can be as creative as you like, choosing colours to match or contrast with your pony's browband and your tie or hair ribbons, for example.

17 Equipment head

A. *Crêpe paper* **B.** *Glass* **C.** *Card* **D.** *Stapler* **E.** *Glue*
F. *Scissors* **G.** *Pen* **H.** *Felt* **I.** *Ribbon* **J.** *Paper fastener* **K.** *Ruler*

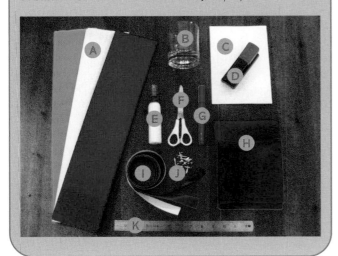

How to make a rosette

With a ruler and pen mark out a strip of crêpe paper for the outer circle of your rosette. Try to make it about 36in (90cm) long and 4in (10cm) wide. Carefully cut this strip out and fold it tightly in a concertina-fashion **(1)**. When you get to the end, use a staple to hold the folds in place **(2)**.

Fan out the folded strip into a complete circle and staple the outer ends together **(3)**. Now make the second, smaller circle, in the same way, using a strip of crêpe paper about 3in (7cm) wide in a different colour.

Be warned!

These rosettes are not suitable for wearing outside if it's raining. Apart from the fact that the paper and card will go soggy, the colour in the crêpe paper will run if it gets wet, and could stain your clothes.

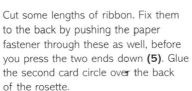

Next cut out two circles of card. Draw round the base of a glass as a guide. Glue the felt circle on to one of the cards. Assemble the rosette, with the felt-covered card on the front. Push a brass paper fastener through the layers **(4)**.

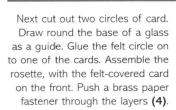

Cut some lengths of ribbon. Fix them to the back by pushing the paper fastener through these as well, before you press the two ends down **(5)**. Glue the second card circle over the back of the rosette.

Attach a safety pin to the back so you can fix the rosette to your jacket. Use a strip of tape to fix the pin to the card **(6)**.

Don't worry if your piece of crêpe paper isn't quite as long as 36 (90cm). It only means that the final rosette will not be quite so full and frilly.

4

School rules

Training your pony to be obedient and responsive will enable you to get twice as much enjoyment out of each other—whether you are hacking, on a fun ride, or competing at championships. It is also important for safety reasons—when riding on roads, especially, you must be sure that your pony will do as he is asked.

Easy as ABC

Mention the word dressage or flatwork and many riders—and their ponies—groan. But dressage is simply teaching your pony to be balanced and responsive, and this makes him far easier and nicer to ride. Riding a balanced, responsive pony is like being driven around in a powerful car that accelerates, brakes, and turns easily and smoothly, which is much more comfortable than being driven in one that rattles your bones! So whether you want to be a happy hacker or a top cross-country rider, dressage can help to make all your riding more enjoyable.

Testing progress
Dressage competitions are a great way of testing out how well you are training your pony. A dressage test is made up of different movements, and a judge gives you a mark out of ten for each movement. The judge will also write comments beside each mark to help you understand which bits you are doing well and where you need to practise more.

Finely tuned
Even a complicated movement such as this canter pirouette is taught simply by improving the horse's balance and responsiveness. A well-schooled pony will learn to wait and listen for your instructions—the aids you give him—and will then perform that movement. First teach him the basic instructions—*see* pages 61–62—and go from there.

Think tall!
Serious dressage riders use a dressage saddle, which helps them to sit in a tall, elegant position. As your balance improves try riding with your stirrups a little longer than usual so that your legs can stretch down and wrap round more of your pony's tummy. Have a picture in your mind of a tall, elegant dressage rider, dressed in top hat and tails, and ride as if you were one.

Showing your approval

The most important part of training your pony is to remember to reward him when he does, or is trying to do, the right thing. Your pony can learn and improve only if he knows when he is right and when he is wrong. Most of us are very quick to let a pony know he is wrong, but he will learn far more—and be far more willing to please you—if you use your voice or a pat to praise him for being good. Remember, also, that many ponies refuse to do the right thing only because they do not understand the instruction, so make sure you are not causing the problem by confusing him.

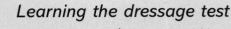

Learning the dressage test

If you are going to enter a dressage competition you will need to learn the test that you are going to ride. Be careful not to practise the whole test too often on your pony or he will very quickly learn it as well and may then start to carry out the next movement before you tell him to. Learn the test by drawing the movements on a sheet of paper, then practise the individual movements on your pony. Don't make practise sessions too long or your pony may become bored and lose the sparkle from his performance. Mix short sessions of training for the test with different, more relaxing exercises that you both enjoy doing.

Practise makes perfect
Working quietly with your pony at home is the best way to put into practise anything you have learnt together recently. You will be more relaxed if no one is watching you.

Make your own arena

If you do not have an arena, you can mark off a suitable area using poles. If possible, use the corner of a field: then the hedge or fence can act as two of the arena's sides.

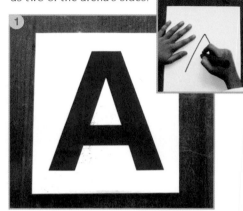

Now you will need to make the letters that are used as marker points around the arena (*see* opposite). Print them out from a computer or draw the letters using a strong black marker (**1**). Color the letters in.

I'll be the judge

Practise different dressage tests at home in front of a friend. Take it in turns to judge each other. Use some old dressage tests—they tell you how many marks to give for good and bad movements. It's all for fun so learn from each other—don't argue with each other!

Learn your letters

It is easier to ride a dressage test if you know where each marker letter is. You may remember them more easily if you think of trotting from Antelope to Elephant instead of from A to E.

Collect old 1-gallon (5-litre) bottles of the rectangular rather than round type. On one side of each container, cover the flat surface with glue and then stick one of your letter cards to it.

He won't go

How often have you seen someone sitting on a pony, kicking and kicking with their heels, and going nowhere? Ponies learn to ignore their riders if they are not taught to listen to their rider's instructions. They may also give up responding if their rider's instructions are confusing. Dressage helps the rider learn to give clearer aids, and teaches the pony to respond accurately. When you are not asking your pony to do something, rest your legs gently against his sides. Use your legs firmly when you do want to give an aid. See pages 64–65 for how to teach your pony to listen to you.

When the glue is dry, fill the bottle with water (**3**) or sand. The weight will prevent it from being toppled by the wind. Replace the lid securely. Now lay out your marked bottles in your home-made arena.

Easy as ABC

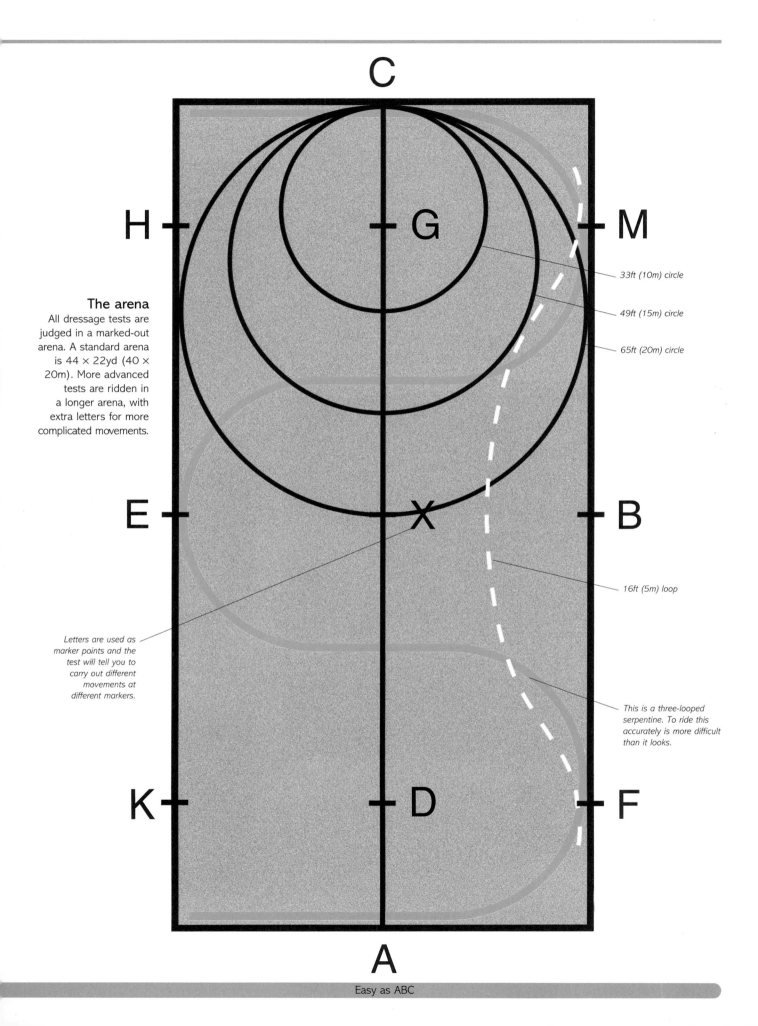

C

H   **G**   **M**

33ft (10m) circle

49ft (15m) circle

65ft (20m) circle

The arena
All dressage tests are judged in a marked-out arena. A standard arena is 44 × 22yd (40 × 20m). More advanced tests are ridden in a longer arena, with extra letters for more complicated movements.

E   **X**   **B**

16ft (5m) loop

Letters are used as marker points and the test will tell you to carry out different movements at different markers.

This is a three-looped serpentine. To ride this accurately is more difficult than it looks.

K   **D**   **F**

A

Dressage games

The following ideas will help you to teach your pony to listen more closely to what you ask him to do. The aim is to teach him to respond quickly and quietly to your instructions, which you give using your legs, hands, and voice. This will allow you to improve his balance and rhythm, which is the secret of all good riding. As your balance improves, you will find it easier to give clearer aids with legs and hands.

Rein contact

Keeping a soft but constant contact with your pony's mouth is one of the secrets of good riding. Ask a friend to draw the rein backwards and forwards to mimic the movement of your pony's head and neck. Relax your elbows so you follow the movement without letting the reins slacken.

⭐ Listen to my legs!

Use your voice and a firm squeeze with your legs to ask your pony to move forwards. If he doesn't respond repeat the action but at the same time tap him behind your leg with the schooling whip. When he does move forward, remember to pat him.

Neck strap

The harder you pull on the reins the more your pony will pull against you. To break the habit use a neck strap instead of the reins to give the command to slow or halt. (Make one out of an old stirrup leather.)

Ride in walk. Put the reins in one hand and hold the neck strap with the other. While keeping a steady feel on the reins, use your legs and voice to ask the pony to halt.

If your pony doesn't stop, continue to use your legs and voice but now pull hard on the neck strap until he stops. Then release the strap and make a big fuss of him.

Rhythm and balance

Looking ahead

You should always be planning what you are going to do next by looking ahead to see where the marker is for the next movement. That way you will be well-prepared to carry it out in good time.

Lovely legs

There is a right and a wrong way for you to use your legs when you are asking your pony to do things and it's important that you learn the correct way and don't get into bad habits. To use your legs properly, relax your knee and then let it come away from the saddle a little. Then squeeze INWARDS, just behind your pony's girth, with the back of your lower leg. DON'T just slide your leg back. Squeeze inwards and you will see why so many riders end up being a bit bow-legged! But this is the right way to do it!

Practise everything that you have learnt by keeping the same rhythm and balance while you trot a perfect circle over four poles laid out on the ground. Make sure that you ride the same number of strides between each pole, and always aim to cross the same part of each pole.

Correct   Incorrect

Don't give up!

Be strict with yourself: Make sure that you ask your pony to do things properly. He must understand that you won't give up until he listens to you. Remember that you can use your voice, your legs, the neck strap, and the schooling whip to encourage him to respond. However, do always make sure you are being fair to your pony by making your instructions clear: ask your instructor to watch you.

5

Jumping for fun

Learning to jump your pony is a perfect way to enjoy the partnership you share. For both pony and rider, happy jumping comes down to having complete confidence in each other. Take it all one step at a time and keep everything small so that you gradually build up your own confidence as well as that of your pony. Then you'll be a fearless team!

Ready for take-off

Jumping should be fun for both you and your pony. Remember that it is your pony that actually does the jumping—your job is to keep him balanced, in a good rhythm, and heading in the right direction! The following exercises will show you that if you stick to your job and don't interfere with your pony, he will get on and do the jumping for you. If you get the approach right then the jump is easy.

Pole on a circle
Practise keeping your pony balanced and in a rhythm by simply trotting on a circle over a pole on the ground. Aim for the centre of the pole each time, keeping the rhythm (*see* page 65).

Strong legs

Strong legs help you keep your balance. Learn to keep your weight in your heel and your leg still. Strengthen your legs by standing up in the stirrups while trotting. Let your knee and ankle joints soak up your pony's up-and-down movement.

Angled poles
In competitive jumping you sometimes have to ride to a fence at an angle. Practise this by putting two poles on the ground and trotting and cantering over them at an angle. Put a mark on each pole so you have a target to aim for.

Sitting pretty

Your body should move as little as possible when jumping. If you can sit quietly and securely in the saddle then your pony can keep his balance and you can keep yours. Just let your hands and shoulders come forward a little to follow the movement of your pony's head. Keep your weight pushed down into your heels and your lower leg close against your pony's sides. Look up and ahead, in the direction you are going, not at the jump or at the ground. Some riders throw their bodies forwards as if they have got to do the jumping. Just as the poor pony tries to take off, they jump up his neck, weighing him down and making it difficult for him to balance. For a safe, secure position, keep your seat and lower leg close to your pony.

Correct position

Incorrect position

Let the pony do the jumping!

See how uncomfortable—and unsafe—it looks if you jump right out of the saddle. It wouldn't take much for this rider to fall off, despite the fact that his pony is jumping very nicely.

Riding circles over a pole

When riding circles, concentrate on keeping the balance and rhythm. With your inside hand ask your pony to look slightly to the inside as this will help him stay on a true circle. It is also helpful to think of turning your own body to point in the direction you are going. So when circling to the right let your shoulders and hips turn slightly to the right. When circling to the left turn your body slightly to the left. Aim for the centre of the pole each time. Once you have got the idea of trotting over a pole on a circle, try doing it in canter.

Inside and outside

When schooling, the words inside and outside, rather than left and right, are often used. The inside leg, hand, rein, and so on, is the one on the inside of the pony's bend. So if you are circling left, your inside leg is the left one, your outside leg the right one.

Circle exercise

Now we are ready to jump. Replace the pole on a circle with a small jump. Ask a friend to stand in the middle of the circle. Canter around on the circle concentrating on keeping the same rhythm and balance. As you get near to the jump keep riding in just the same way but look across to your friend in the middle of the circle.

⭐ No cheating

To make sure you don't cheat and sneak a peek at the jump, ask your friend to hold up a different number of fingers each time you jump. On the way to the jump, look across and say how many fingers are being shown. Once you have got used to simply keeping in the same rhythm and waiting for the jump, you can try without looking away: Even then, it helps to look to the other side of the jump rather than at it.

By looking at your friend, not the jump, you won't be tempted to interfere with your pony. Keep riding him in the same rhythm and balance, and before you know it you will have jumped the jump!

Angled jump

Having mastered cantering at an angle over poles on the ground, you can now turn them into angled jumps.	Decide the line you are going to ride and look up and ahead to something in the distance that will keep you on that line.	Having cleared the first jump make sure you use your hands and legs to keep your pony going at the same angle.	After the final jump, ride away at the same angle for a few strides to teach your pony to stay on the line you ask for.

Jump positions

Short strides

Once you have learned to canter a circle over a jump while keeping an even rhythm, ask your pony to lengthen and then shorten his stride. Shorten it by keeping a stronger contact on the reins; lengthen it by relaxing the contact so your pony stretches his body. Use the "No Cheating" exercise (see page 71) to try this out. When cantering on a short stride the pony will usually take off closer to the jump.

Take-off: Just allow your shoulders and hands to go forward a little to follow your pony's movement as he takes off. Keep your bottom close to the saddle and keep a soft feel on the reins. This rider has come too far out of the saddle!

Long strides

Cantering on a longer stride means your pony will usually take off further away from the jump. Both this rider, and the one top right, have lifted themselves too far out of the saddle on take-off, which is a common mistake. Try to relax your body, and don't try to guess what your pony is going to do.

Mid-air: Hold your position so that your weight stays over the center of your pony, not behind or in front of it. Look ahead to where you are going, not down toward the landing. Keep your bottom in the saddle and your weight pushed down on your heels.

3

Landing: As your pony's front feet touch the ground you must bring your shoulders back up to the upright position so that your weight remains central. You will then be sitting correctly when your pony canters on to the next fence. Remember to keep the soft feel on the reins. It is often at take-off and landing that the rider's hands do not properly follow the movement of the pony's head; there is then a risk of jabbing the pony's mouth.

Practise makes perfect

Good jumping takes time and effort. Be patient and keep practising the basics until you feel you have a secure, well-balanced position when jumping. Keep practising the circle exercise over small jumps until you feel really confident about keeping the same rhythm all the way to the jump, and about relaxing your body so that you stay in balance with your pony.

Grid games

Gridwork involves jumping a number of fairly low fences in succession. It is a way of giving your pony an athletic workout over jumps—a bit like you having a workout at the gymnasium. It helps him to become better at jumping and more athletic generally and it is a good way of improving your balance and reactions. It can also help you to understand how to judge your pony's stride and make adjustments where necessary.

Setting up the course
You will need someone to help you set up and adjust the grid (line of jumps) so that the distances between jumps are correct for the work you are doing. This will help your pony to improve his jumping. If the distances are wrong you and your pony will soon lose confidence.

Put a spring in his step!
Give your pony extra spring by working out over some grids.

Lengthening the stride

The distance between each jump can be adjusted to teach your pony to shorten and lengthen his stride and his jump. Here the pony takes a long stride in the middle and has to take off quite a long way from the jump.

Shortening the stride

In the grid the two jumps have been moved about 1ft 6in (0.5m) closer together. This makes the pony take a shorter stride, which in turn makes him take off closer to the second jump.

Short and neat
This grid has two spread fences with one stride between them. You can gradually make the spread fences wider by moving the jump stands in towards each other. This shortens the distance in the middle, teaching your pony to shorten his body and stride.

Jump to it!

If you and your pony enjoy jumping there are all sorts of competitions you can take part in. The different classes are decided either by the height of your pony, or by the amount of prizes or money he has won in previous competitions. Open classes are open to all horses and ponies. You can start by jumping very small courses; if you are good enough you can build up to riding at the most important and difficult competitions. Most competitions involve jumping a first round, followed by a jump-off between all those who jumped clear in the first round. In the jump-off the jumps are higher and the fastest clear round wins.

Learn from others

Spend some time watching how other riders tackle the course. Jumps are often set up on difficult distances so you have to decide whether to go for a few long strides or more short strides. Decide which will suit your pony best.

Aim high!

If you and your pony are successful showjumpers then you can find yourself competing at the biggest shows in the country. There are national and international competitions for junior riders, so set your sights high.

Look this way

We are taught to look up and in the direction we want to go when we are riding and jumping. In the competitive showjumping arena, the horse must make quick changes of direction and pace in order to complete a course efficiently in the shortest possible time, so the rider must be able to think well ahead and must therefore learn to look around to where the next jump is, not to where the horse will land. This rider is looking to see where she has to go next.

Stepping out

Pace the distance between the fences to work out the number of pony strides between each. The average pony's canter stride is about 10ft (3m); work out how many of your own strides equal this.

Don't hang on

If you fall off, it is important to let go of the reins and curl up into a ball. If you try to hang on to the reins (as the rider in the picture is trying to do) you may pull your pony on top of you. He won't want to tread on you but if he can't get away he might hurt you accidentally.

Quick turn

In a jump-off every second counts and could be the difference between winning or losing. Practise jumping so that you land with your pony going in the direction of the next fence. In mid-air, start to turn his head and your own body in that direction.

DIY jumping

Most of us aren't lucky enough to own a full set of showjumps to practise with at home. But if you can collect one or two jump stands and some garbage cans or barrels you can use your imagination to put together a small course. Get an experienced adult to check that anything you plan to use will not cause serious injury should your pony hit it or fall on to it.

Get building
Building a course can be fun, but have it checked for safety, and make sure it is laid out with sensible distances between each jump.

Building a course at home
For this you need a fairly large area of grass or a riding arena. If ou are using a field or paddock, first check that there are no holes, tree roots or other hazards that could injure your pony. Once you have it set up, try approaching the course in different ways. Here, two routes over the jumps are shown. If you have very few materials, build just the angled double and the corner.

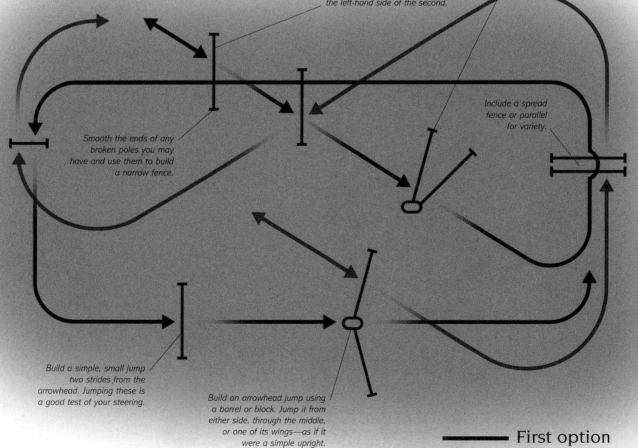

Set two jumps at an angle to each other, with one stride between. Jump from either direction, at an angle or n a straight line, keeping to the right-hand side of the first jump and the left-hand side of the second.

Build a corner jump from two poles placed on a barrel or block to form a point. Jump it from either direction. Put it in line with the angled double.

Smooth the ends of any broken poles you may have and use them to build a narrow fence.

Include a spread fence or parallel for variety.

Build a simple, small jump two strides from the arrowhead. Jumping these is a good test of your steering.

Build an arrowhead jump using a barrel or block. Jump it from either side, through the middle, or one of its wings—as if it were a simple upright.

—— First option
—— Second option

Club together

Showjumps are expensive, especially if you buy them new rather than secondhand, but if you can acquire a few it will be well worth it. If you want to compete often, you will certainly need access to a course that you can practise on between competitions. Why not get together with friends and buy some jumps between you. If you keep them all at the same place you can all practise over all of them.

Painting poles

To save money you can often buy rustic showjumping poles (poles that haven't been painted), or secondhand poles whose paint has worn off. Buy some tins of paint, or see what odds and ends you have lying around at home. Then get out your paintbrush and redesign them in bright colors and patterns.

Right on target

Use some tape to mark the center of each pole. You can then aim for this when you are jumping. You can also use tape to mark the points to aim for when you are doing the angled jumps exercise (see page 71).

Plastic jumps

There are many different designs of jump stand available, and some of the safest and easiest to use are plastic ones. As seen here, you can buy plastic blocks, which are used instead of uprights to support the poles, as well as shaped wings. Plastic blocks and wings are more robust than traditional wooden jump stands in that they do not rot or deteriorate in wet weather or hot sun. They therefore do not require so much care and maintenance to keep them safe and usable. They are also lighter and easier to move from one part of the course to another.

Now do it!
You've practised how to sit properly, how to ride a good approach, how to stay straight and balanced. Now it should all come together in a perfect jump. Aim to keep your seat in the saddle and your weight in your heels, looking up and ahead.

Jumping games

As well as practising your jumping skills by riding over courses and grids, and doing specific exercises, you can play some jumping games with your friends to add to the fun. They are just as good a way of improving your riding and your pony's skills without either of you feeling under pressure. It's a game, so don't take it too seriously. It doesn't really matter who wins as long as you all enjoy yourselves.

Narrow fences and blocks

To ride accurately over a really narrow fence such as a single block, your pony has to understand that he really is meant to jump over the thing you have aimed at. Keep a good contact on the reins and concentrate on keeping his whole body, his head and his neck really straight. Keep your own body and head straight, too. Don't go fast—just approach steadily in an even rhythm aiming for the middle of the block.

Chase me Charlie

This is a fun game for a group of riders. Put up a small jump. Follow each other over it one at a time. When everyone has jumped it once, raise the jump a hole. Anyone who knocks it down is out of the game. Continue in this way, putting the jump up each time, until there is only one person left who can jump it. (If you can persuade an assistant or two to move the pole each time, so much the better.)

Accuracy

Get in some practise before you try the block or barrel elimination game (see opposite). Put a block on the ground with two poles as wings to funnel your pony towards the block. Once he understands he is meant to jump the single block, try removing the poles.

Jumping games

Block- or barrel-elimination game

1

2

3

This is a "knock-out" game that works on the same principle as "Chase me Charlie." Put down a line of barrels or blocks to form a jump. Follow each other over the jump one at a time.

When everyone has jumped the line of blocks, take one away to make the jump narrower. All jump it again. If your pony runs out or knocks the blocks over you are out. Better luck next time!

After each round, take another block away. If you are really good you will get right down to jumping over one barrel. To help everyone, have a practise first using one block with poles as wings.

Off to the show

Spending a day out at a show on a warm sunny day is one of the best ways of having fun with your pony. There is something for everyone, from specialist shows that have only one type of class to general shows that have every class you can think of—gymkhanas, showjumping, showing, dressage, and even fancy dress.

Choosing your class

Shows are divided into classes for different breeds, such as Mountain and Moorland breeds, or for different types of horse and pony, such as first-ridden, show hunter, and working hunter. There may be further divisions based on size, such as small or large hunter, or lightweight, middleweight, or heavyweight. Equitation classes are judged on how well you ride rather than on how your pony looks or acts.

Ask advice

It takes experience to know which class would be best for your pony to enter. If there is no one to advise you before the show, don't be afraid to ask a judge or another competitor at the show what they think your pony should compete in.

Lead-rein class
Ponies in this class must show they are safe and suitable mounts for children not yet ready to ride on their own. The judge looks for good manners, and overall smartness and calmness—so this includes the rider and whoever is leading them!

★ Ringcraft

To win prizes you have to try to show your pony off at his best in the ring. This is called ringcraft. When everyone is parading together, make sure you don't move too close to the next competitor: Keep enough space around you so that the judge can see you. If you are getting too close to the pony in front, and the one behind is too close to you, just circle away from the line and rejoin the parade where there is more room.

In-hand class

Ponies are not ridden in this class but led in front of the judge in walk and trot. The pony is judged on his manners, conformation, and turnout.

Judges' line-up

The whole class parades before the judge in walk, trot, and canter. The judge lines up the ponies in order, best first. Each then performs an individual show, and the judge decides on the final order of placings.

First-ridden

Ponies in this class have to show that they are suitable rides for children who are just starting to ride on their own. So it is important that they are calm, well-mannered, and cooperative.

★ Keep it simple

When giving an individual show for the judge, try to picture an arena so that you ride within a limited space and don't go wandering miles from the judge. Keep it short and simple—do more in the pace your pony is best at and less in the pace he finds hardest.

Sideways on

If you enjoy riding side-saddle why not join a side-saddle association. They hold their own shows and championships. If you can ride side-saddle it is a good way of standing out from the crowd in normal showing classes as well!

Mountain and Moorland showing classes

Mountain and Moorland breeds may be judged separately as individual breeds or together in a Mountain and Moorland class. These breeds are shown in a natural state, so their manes and tails should not be pulled or plaited, and heels should not be trimmed.

All dressed up

If you like dressing up then you can compete in Concours d'Elegance classes or, for a bit of fun, in fancy dress classes.

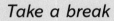

Take a break

If you are lined up in a large class and the weather is very hot, it can be a good idea to get off your pony's back while you are waiting to give your show. Don't wait until the last minute to get back on—remount while there are a few left to go.

Working hunters

In working-hunter classes your pony will have to jump a course of rustic jumps. Sometimes, only those that go clear are allowed to go through to the final judging.

Away days

To really enjoy a day out at a show you do need to plan ahead and get organized. It is a good idea to pack everything you need the day before. This way you will have time to rush out and buy anything you find you have run out of. There should also be time to clean anything that may have been overlooked since the last day out. You need to think of what you would like with you to make it a fun day out, and what to take to make it fun for your pony too. Play safe and take more, not less, than you need.

Get packing
A happy pony needs a well-organized owner. Make a list of what to pack—for your pony as well as you.

Blankets
When traveling inside a vehicle your pony can become quite hot. He may not need a blanket at all if it is very hot although a light cotton blanket will keep the dust off his coat and protect him from the sun. Any traveling blanket should be made of breathable material. These are called coolers.

Travel kit
If you are likely to go to lots of shows it is worth keeping some of your equipment especially for days out so that it is always clean and in good condition. A set of grooming brushes and a favorite blanket are good things to keep just for outings.

Poll guard

Some ponies throw their heads around when they are traveling, particularly when they are being loaded up the ramp. A poll guard is a specially shaped pad that protects the top of your pony's head from injury.

Travel boots

You can buy specially shaped boots to protect your pony's legs when he is traveling. Travel boots help prevent cuts and bruises if he loses his balance and either treads on himself or bangs against the side of the trailer. If you don't have boots then use stable wraps with thick padding underneath on all his legs.

Checklist

Keep a permanent list of the things you need to remember to take every time you have a day out with your pony. Keep it somewhere safe so that you always know where to find it. Always check the list and get everything ready the day before.

- Saddle, bridle, spare headcollar, and rope. Girths, saddle blankets, and any protective boots (in addition to traveling ones) that you might want to use for warming up or for jumping.

- Containers of water, buckets, sponges, towels, and sweat-scrapers.

- Your riding clothing—hat, jacket, shirt, tie or stock, jodhpurs, boots, and spurs if needed. Gloves and whip. And don't forget your body protector.

- The schedule, directions, and any rule book appropriate for the show you are going to. If the show is fairly local, it can be worth taking a list of useful phone numbers, including the vet's and the farrier's.

- Food and drink for you and your family and any fans!

- Haynet, and extra hay and feed for your pony (always take more than you need in case of a breakdown or unexpected delay).

- Selection of spare rugs, including something waterproof if you have it as you never know what the weather may do.

- First-aid kit for horses and humans

- Grooming kit, braiding equipment (to redo any braids that work loose), saddle soap and polish, spare sponges for that final tidy-up.

- Last—but not least—don't forget to load up your pony. People have arrived at a show with everything except the horse!

On the day

A day at a show should be fun, but you should also make the most of the opportunity to learn as much as you can by watching other classes and riders. Don't forget that it is a long day for your pony as well, and he will need a rest and perhaps a wash-off and drink between classes. Always allow plenty of time to arrive and get ready—none of us is at our best when we are in a rush.

Show plan

If your class lets you have an individual show plan, practise it in advance. Use some dressage test movements. Leave anything your pony finds difficult until the end so any mistakes you might make won't upset too much of your show.

Rest time

Get off your pony's back when you are able to so that you can both take a break. If it is hot try to stand him in some shade.

Pretty in tweed

This tidy little rider is wearing a tweed hacking jacket, which can be worn with a shirt and tie or with a hunting tie.

Dark and smart

A dark blue or black show jacket can be worn instead of a tweed jacket. This does look very smart and grown-up and can also be worn in the hunting field.

Well led

In some classes you will have to take your pony's saddle off and lead him past the judge in walk and trot. Take the reins over your pony's head and try to stay level with his neck. You should always lead your pony on your left hand side (near side). Practise leading your pony up at home. It is important that he walks and trots willingly beside you. Carry a schooling whip in your right hand and give him a little tap with it to ask him to trot on. Use your voice at the same time so that he learns to respond to you saying "trot on."

Prim and proper

Different types of show have different rules on turnout (how you and your horse should look). The rules also vary according to the type of pony you have and the type of class he is entered in. Don't be afraid to ask other people or to call the show secretary to find out what is expected. Whatever show you are entering, pay special attention to those final details. These details might make all the difference on the day—and, what's more, it's great fun!

Applying baby oil
You can make the soft skin around your pony's nose and eyes look really sleek and shiny by rubbing a small amount of baby oil on it.

Some ponies are ridden in a double bridle. It takes practise to use both reins correctly and kindly.

Mane plaits
Before braiding your pony's mane (or tail) for a show, check he is not a type that should be shown with his mane and tail left loose and unpulled (see page 91). If you braid them, get rid of tangles first. A mane must be "pulled" before you braid (see pages 30-31).

Whiskers
Your pony uses the whiskers around his muzzle to sense and feel what is around him. This is especially important as he cannot actually see what is under his nose! So while it is tempting to trim the whiskers off, it is kinder to leave them as they are. If you really have to trim them off, ask an adult to do it carefully for you. They should use a disposable plastic razor or a small set of clippers.

Fancy footwork
Using a comb and scissors, carefully trim the long hair around your pony's heels. Start with the hairs highest up the leg and use the comb to light them clear of your pony's legs. With the scissors pointing downwards, trim the hairs that stick through the comb. Brush hoof oil or lotion on to his feet to keep them healthy and shiny.

Trimming the tail

Your pony uses his tail to swish off flies so you should never cut it off short. A good length is about 7.5cm (3in) below his hocks. Your pony will hold his tail up slightly when moving, so watch him walking to see how high he carries it. You can then make allowance for this when trimming it: Hold the tail at the height he carries it, and then decide how much to cut off.

Don't forget your own turnout. Make sure your clothes are clean and tidy and your boots are shiny.

Serious stencils

These quarter marks have been produced by using a ready-made stencil pattern. If you don't have a stencil, you can do them by hand, using a small section of comb. See page 29. You can always break off a piece of a plastic hair comb if your mane comb is too big for the pattern you want to make.

Brighten up his legs with chalk, and shine up his hooves with hoof oil.

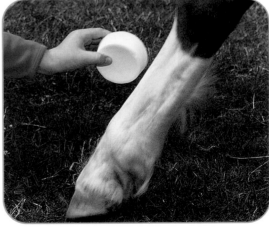

Whiter than white

White markings are hard to keep clean. First wash them with water and shampoo. Once dry you can rub on chalk to make them really bright, but do not do this on his face as the chalk may get into his eyes.

Wet and wild

Enjoying the great outdoors with your pony is great fun for both of you. There are all sorts of activities you can enjoy while exploring the countryside. Long-distance riding, hunting, and fun rides take you miles into the unknown, while cross-country riding and hunter trials teach you to tackle all sorts of challenges, from water jumps to drop fences.

Going the distance

Exploring new areas of the country is a perfect excuse for getting out and about on your pony and, like you, your pony enjoys new sights, sounds and experiences. For the less competitive rider there are sponsored rides, hunting, horsey holidays, and pony trekking. And for those with a competitive edge there are hunter trials, horse trials, and long-distance riding. Try out everything and see which you enjoy the most.

Fit for the job

Make sure you and your pony are reasonably fit before getting too ambitious about how far you are going to travel. Go on longer hacks than normal to build up your fitness together, and then try some fun rides to see how you cope with longer distances.

Over, under, or through

Once you start to explore the great outdoors you will need to be able to cope with various obstacles, such as opening and shutting gates, slip-rails, and so on. This hunter trial competitor shows how to deal with a slip-rail.

Pony trekking

If you don't own a pony why not go pony trekking and enjoy a day out on someone else's pony? There are many pony-trekking centers where you will be taken out riding for a day, or you can go on a week's riding holiday, where you ride out somewhere different every day. You can also opt for a training holiday where you can have concentrated instruction on cross-country riding, showjumping, or whatever particularly interests you.

Sponsored rides

These are organized rides through open countryside with optional jumps on the way round. The aim is to raise money for a good cause or charity while having fun. To take part you have to raise a certain amount of sponsorship money or pledges in advance, or pay a minimal entry fee. They are a good way of getting a feel for longer outings and adventures, and they are good for meeting new horsey people.

Horsey holiday

Why not enjoy a holiday with your pony in a different part of the country. Or, for a change, give your pony a holiday at home and ride the holiday center's ponies.

Crossing the country

Learning to tackle natural obstacles and challenges such as fences, water, ditches, quarries, and varying terrain, is one of the most rewarding and exhilarating ways of enjoying your pony. Whether your ambition is to win the Kentucky or Badminton horse trials, or to go clear at your local hunter trial, you will get huge satisfaction from rising to the challenge of cross-country riding.

Get dressed up!
Your pony will enjoy the challenge of cross-country, but he will need to wear protective clothing just as you do.

Open and shut

Hunter trial courses usually include a gate or slip-rail to negotiate. At home or when out hacking, practise teaching your pony to stand still while you undo gates from the saddle. If the gate opens toward you, your pony must walk backwards a few steps while you pull the gate open. If it opens the other way you just push it open and ride your pony through. Then about turn and shut it again.

Where are we going?

At every hunter trial there should be a map of the course. Study it carefully. There are usually different color flags for different classes or levels. Always walk the course as well—the map is just a guide.

Walk the course!

If there is time, walk the course twice. First time round, work out what the jumps are like and where they are on the course, and look out for anything that may cause difficulties. Second time round, walk the exact route you are going to ride, allowing for taking different options at different fences.

Get fit!

To ride safely and successfully across country, you and your pony both need to be fit. Build fitness gradually by doing a little bit more cantering when you are out hacking and choosing longer, hillier rides so that your pony has to work a bit harder each time. Improve your own strength and stamina by doing exercises out of the saddle.

Chocoholic

Hunts are very demanding. They normally meet mid-morning and continue hunting until dusk. You and your pony will probably be tired out before then but to help you on your way, a bar of chocolate tucked in your pocket will soon lift your energy levels. It will also make you very popular!

Happy hunting

Hunting is a great way to learn how to cope with whatever the natural terrain has to throw at you. The horses and riders follow the hounds. Because no one knows which way the hunted animal will run you never know where you will be heading next. It teaches you to have very quick reactions and good balance.

It's a long way…

Long-distance riding is a test of fitness and horsemanship. You follow a set route (between 25 and 100 miles/40–160km), with veterinary checks along the way. The aim is to complete the route with a horse who is still happy and healthy.

Cross-country kit

Whenever you ride you should always wear a proper riding hat or helmet. But to ride over cross-country jumps you need a bit more protection. Because the fences are solid there is the risk that your pony may actually fall if he hits one, you may be thrown against a solid fence, and your pony can knock his legs against the fence as well. Wearing the correct protection will reduce the risk of injury to both of you.

Well protected
A body protector cannot guarantee that you won't get hurt if you fall but it certainly reduces the chance of your upper body being seriously injured. It needs to be close-fitting but not so tight that you cannot move naturally in it.

A well-fitting riding helmet made to the highest safety standards is essential for cross-country riding.

A body protector with shoulder pads will help to protect your collar bones in the event of a fall.

★ Replace your kit
If you have a bad fall it is best to replace both your hat and body protector before you ride again. You may not see any damage but a heavy blow to the protective material in both will make them weaker and less protective should you fall off again.

Long sleeves will help protect your arms from scratches and grazes. But don't get overheated—in very hot weather wear something lighter underneath the body protector.

Wear non-slip gloves so that you can keep a good grip on the reins.

Pony protection

Your pony needs special equipment, too. Leg boots or wraps will help protect his legs should he hit a fence; overreach boots will protect the heels of his front feet if the hind feet strike them (as they can do when jumping and galloping). A safety girth will help hold the saddle on, and a martingale will stop your pony from throwing his head too high.

A safety girth, or overgirth, goes right round the saddle and over the normal girth. It is a safety measure in case the saddle's girth or girth straps break.

Some ponies get very strong and excited across country—a martingale will stop your pony's head getting too high, and you may need a stronger bit than for normal riding.

Sticky tape on top of boot straps or bandage ties reduces the chance of them working loose.

Overreach boots protect the pony's heels from damage that can be inflicted by the back hooves.

Bottom up!

When riding cross-country it is easier for your pony to carry you—and for you to keep your balance—if you keep your bottom out of the saddle. So have your stirrups shorter than usual. Try riding in the position shown by the girl on the grey pony here.

Hold hard

When riding cross-country it is more important than ever that you keep a nice feel on the reins so that you can help balance your pony should he stumble. Keep a feel on his mouth over the fence as well as when riding between fences. Loose, flappy reins won't help him at all if he makes a mistake.

Practise makes perfect

Before trying out the challenges of solid cross-country fences you can practise many of the maneuvers by using showjumps at home. For inspiration, walk round a few cross-country courses to see how you could adapt your jumps at home. Tests such as bounces, corners, and arrowheads can easily be copied at home.

Film star
Ask someone to video you when you are jumping. You can then study it to see if you really are doing all the right things or if there are areas you need to work on.

Bounce fences
Your pony will have to land over one jump and immediately take off over another one. At big events such as Kentucky Horse Trials the horses may have to "bounce" over two jumps and then land in water.

Keep your bottom in the saddle and your legs pressed against your pony's sides so you can ask him to take off over the second jump.

Look up and ahead beyond the second part of the bounce so that you keep your balance and keep riding forward in a rhythm.

Narrow double

As soon as your pony's feet land after jumping the first part of the bounce, he has to take off straight away to jump the second part.

A common cross-country challenge is two jumps not completely in line with each other. As in these pictures, you have to aim for the right-hand edge of the first one and the left-hand edge of the second.

As you land over the first one, keep your head up and look straight down the line you are riding, not directly at the fence. If you lose concentration at this point your pony may be tempted to run out.

Use your legs and hands to keep your pony straight so that he jumps the second part of the double exactly where you want him to. Make sure your body is straight and not leaning to one side or the other.

Keep looking ahead and riding forward in a straight line as you land over the second part of the jump. This will teach him to keep going in the same direction until you instruct him to change it.

Practising narrow doubles

Narrow doubles can be more challenging than they might seem because it is too easy for the pony to run out to the side of the jump. When first practising this sort of jump, it may help to ask someone to stand well clear of the jump but on the same line as you are riding. This will give you something to aim at. The helper can also tell you if you are wandering a little rather than really sticking to your line.

Getting your feet wet

Take every chance when out riding to ride through puddles and over small ditches so that your pony becomes happy and confident about going through water and over ditches.

Corner fences

This type of fence is found on many courses. Make one at home using a block, barrel, or upturned plastic bin to form the point of the corner.

Make it easy!

When showing your pony a new jumping challenge, make it as easy as possible for him to do the right thing. Here, poles are used as wings to guide the pony from one narrow edge of the jump to the next. Once he understands, they can be taken away.

Up and down

Cross-country courses follow the natural landscape and so will go up and down hills and through whatever else the countryside has to offer. When cantering uphill, make it easier for your pony by lifting your bottom further out of the saddle and bringing your shoulders further forward to keep the weight off his hindquarters.

Arrow heads

These are another popular test of accuracy. Use a block or barrel to form the arrowhead and then place guiding poles either side. Jump it first with the poles helping to funnel you in and then come from the other direction and see if you can still keep your pony on target.

Ditches

Lay a strip of plastic sheeting on the floor and weigh it down with two poles. You can fold it up to be very narrow to start with and then open it out to mimic a wider ditch once your pony is happy with it.

Ponies take great confidence if given a lead by another person or pony. By getting someone to walk over the plastic, you are showing your pony that there is nothing for him to be scared of.

Coffin

A coffin combination is a fence that has a ditch in the middle and a solid fence either side of it. Once you are confident about jumping the ditch you can build a fence one stride away on either side. You can also make it a bounce so you land over the first part, take off straight away over the ditch, and take off again over the final part.

Use your hands and legs to keep your pony straight and moving forward in a collected canter up to the first part of the obstacle. Allow your pony time to work out what he has to do.

Look up and over the ditch—never down into it!—and keep riding forward in a straight line to the final element.

If he still looks worried about it, get a more experienced pony to jump it ahead of him. This pony pricks his ears and looks at the "ditch" but he knows it's nothing to be afraid of and is ready to jump.

He jumps cleanly over the ditch, showing the more nervous pony how things are done. This rider should try to keep his bottom closer to the saddle to keep a safe, secure seat, like the rider in the next picture.

Now the younger pony tries for himself. Because he is still a little unsure he has jumped much higher than he needs to. Just keep jumping the ditch backwards and forwards until your pony is condfident.

Keep a good but not hard contact with your pony's mouth by not allowing the reins to go slack. This gives him confidence and keeps him moving in the direction you want.

Copy cats

Be inspired by the challenges and questions that you see being asked set at major horse trials and competitions. The fences themselves may seem elaborate and complex but look to see exactly what it is that they are asking the horse and rider to do. With a little bit of imagination you should be able to imitate many of these at home.

Ditch and turn

The rider below is at Badminton Horse Trials, in the UK, and has to jump a wide ditch and then turn sharp right to another jump. The environment is very different, but the rider above right is doing exactly the same thing!

Home-made style

You can practise doing the jump shown below by putting your plastic ditch on a turn to another fence. As you are in the air over the ditch, you will need to start to turn your pony toward the next jump.

Angled jumps

Cross-country jumps are often set at very sharp angles to each other. This tests the rider's accuracy and the horse's obedience.

Build two jumps at home, set at different angles to each other. Ride a straight line that takes you over the middle of each one.

Your pony will be moving in a straight line but will meet the jumps at an angle. Let him work out when to take off.

Keep it small

While you are learning these new skills and challenges, keep the fences small until you are both really confident. Start with poles on the ground and then build up to whatever height you are happy with.

Keep it slow

When particular accuracy and control is needed, such as to jump an arrowhead, keep your approach slower so you will have more control. If you go too fast your pony may just nip past, instead of over, the jump.

Mushrooms

Cross-country course designers are forever coming up with all sorts of new obstacles to test competitors and entertain spectators. Carved wooden mushrooms are a popular feature on many courses now. In themselves they are no more difficult to jump than most other obstacles, but your pony may be reluctant to have a go simply because they look different from anything he's jumped before. Once again, practise and confidence-building exercises at home are the answer, and it always helps to walk your pony up to a new obstacle and let him inspect it before asking him to jump it. With a little imagination, you can pretend that the obstacle shown here is a mushroom!

Mitsubishi M jump

This is a sponsor's fence at the international Badminton Horse Trials in the UK. It looks complicated but it is really just a double set of corners. Build corners at home, set a couple of strides apart, and pretend you are an international competitor.

As always, ride a good straight line that takes you directly over the portion of the corner that you want to jump. Use your hands and legs to keep your pony on the line. Remember to keep looking ahead in the direction you wish to go.

As with any jump that you do not approach in the center, there is an increased risk that your pony will be tempted to run out to the side of it. Keep a good rein contact and stick to your line until you have landed clear of the second corner.

The real thing

So you have practised as much as you can at home and you've splashed through every puddle and ditch you can find while out hacking. The moment has come to test your ability over the real thing—a proper cross-country course. Make sure you wear all the protective clothing—body protectors can be worn over or under your clothes. Now it's time to sit tight and have some real fun!

Stepping up
Chose a small set of steps to practise over first and approach them in trot to begin with. Once your pony understands what to do, come in canter, keeping a strong, even rhythm. Keep your shoulders up so that you don't weigh down your pony's front end—he needs to lift that up in the air to get up the steps.

Make a splash!
Cross-country riding is demanding, and it might mean getting wet (for you as well as your pony!) But it's great fun.

Helping hands
Always take an adult with you when you go cross-country jumping. If there's a problem, or if you are unlucky enough to have an accident, you will need some help. Ideally, go with one or two friends as well so that the more confident ponies and riders can give the less experienced ones a lead over the jumps.

Good approach
As we have said earlier in this book, good jumping comes down to riding a good approach. That is your job—your pony does the rest.

Ride your pony up into a good strong canter but concentrate on keeping the same rhythm. Keep your head and shoulders up and your legs pressed against your pony's sides.

Trotting

If your pony is very inexperienced at cross-country then start gently. If you go charging over the course before you have introduced him to it you will create problems for the future. Jump the smallest version of all the jumps first. Approach everything in trot so that it is easier to keep him collected and balanced and gives the pony time to work out what he has to do.

Approaching the jump

Taking the jump

Raise your shoulders as your pony drops down off the step.

Stepping down

Having jumped up some steps you can turn round and jump down them as well. Because you are heading downhill it is easier to lose your balance and tip forward too much. Concentrate on keeping your shoulders up and your lower leg pressed against your pony's sides.

As you get closer to take-off, allow your hands and shoulders forward a little, but without losing contact. Press harder with your heels but keep your bottom in the saddle.

Notice how this rider's legs and seat stay in the same line throughout the approach, take-off, and jump. This is what you should aim for—a still, secure but effective position.

Go with the flow

Once you have jumped a variety of obstacles, make up a course and jump several obstacles one after the other. Keep looking up and ahead to where you want to go next.

Keep a good contact with your pony's mouth but be ready to let your hands go forward with his movement so that he can stretch his neck if he needs to.

Drop off

A bank is just a bigger version of the step up and down. Once you feel confident and secure jumping steps, try a bank. Remember to keep your shoulders up when you drop off the top.

Jumping a ditch

If you are worried that a ditch is too wide, remember how much ground your pony covers with each stride of his canter (at least 10ft/3m). He could canter over most ditches without even knowing they were there!

Keep your bottom sitting securely in the saddle as your pony may jump extra wide and high if he is not sure about the ditch

Pretend it's not there!

Try not to let yourself or your pony look down into the bottom of the ditch, as this may frighten you both. Keep your focus up and forward, and just imagine the ditch is the plastic sheet that you practised over at home. If you think nothing of it, then your pony is less likely to worry about it.

Take it easy

Each time you teach your pony to jump a new type of obstacle, make a big fuss of him and then let him go and jump something he is already familiar with. This will keep his confidence high. If you keep setting him difficult tasks without letting him have an easy jump, he may start to lose confidence. This is important because a confident pony can make your job a lot easier—and safer.

Different ditches

Because course designers know that ditches frighten some ponies and riders they do like to use quite a lot of them in different ways to see if they can catch you out. Here, the course designer has created a trekhener—a jump with a ditch underneath it. But in the end, a ditch is simply another jump, however it is used, and if you introduce your pony to different ditches carefully and quietly neither of you will have any reason to be worried. A pony will often take his lead from you, so if you can be calm about ditches your pony will be so, too.

Water babies

Water is something else your pony may be scared of. Let him follow another pony into the water—just walk him in and let him wander around in it until he is relaxed about it. If he wants to put his nose in it, let him, but don't let him get down and roll!

Bounce away

You have tried a bounce at home, so nows you can try it for real across country. Just ride it exactly the same as when you practised at home.

Raise your shoulders as your pony lands over the first part of the bounce so that his front end is nice and light for him to lift up over the second part.

Walking through water

As soon as your pony is happy about walking in and out of water you can try jumping down a small step into water. Keep your shoulders up and your legs on your pony's sides.

You may have to lean right back like this if your pony takes a great big jump, but always keep hold of the reins so you can help balance and steer him. Keep your own head up as well.

As soon as you land, gather up your reins and keep a firm hold on your pony's head as he may stumble when the drag of the water hits his legs. Remember how hard it is for you to walk through water.

The closer your bottom is to the saddle, the safer and more secure you are. It is easier for your pony's balance if you keep your body in the same place all the time. Sit still!

Raise your shoulders again as you land over the second part of the bounce. Squeeze with your legs and keep a good contact so that he canters away to the next fence in an even rhythm.

Don't dive in!

Now it's time to try a bigger drop into water and…oh dear, the rider has started to dive in before her pony has. Always keep your seat in the saddle, to keep your pony's balance as well as your own, and don't let your shoulders fall too far forward or…

This is what happens! The rider has lost her balance and has been thrown right up her pony's neck. There is nothing keeping her on board at all. Luckily her pony kept his head up and has given her some chance of staying on.

The pony has been very helpful and lifted his head and neck, which allows his rider to push herself back into the saddle. If he had stumbled or tripped she would most certainly have taken a ducking. But they are both certainly enjoying themselves!

Well recovered, but if this happens to you don't laugh too much or you will go all weak and wobbly and fall off anyway. We really need to get those legs back in position quickly. Remember to keep your weight in your heels and your legs close to your pony's sides.

Sit up

By keeping her bottom in the saddle, and not letting her shoulders fall too far forward, everything goes more smoothly. Her lower leg should be further forward to keep her really secure but at least she isn't going to get wet this time.

Perfect posture

To work out the right position for jumping, imagine you can draw a straight line from your shoulder through your knee to your toe. Look at photos of yourself jumping to see how close you are to perfection. And remember – practise makes perfect.

Glossary

Above the bit Describes a pony avoiding contact with the rider by lifting his mouth above the level of the rider's hand.
Aids The use of hand, leg, seat, and voice to instruct the horse.
Artificial aids The whip and spurs, used to reinforce the natural aids.

Barrel Horse's body between forearms and loins.
Bars The gap between the molar and incisor teeth. The mouthpiece of the bit rests on the bars.
Behind the bit A pony is behind the bit when he brings his nose towards his chest. This causes him to lose full contact with the rider's hand.
Breaking Early training, when the pony is taught to accept the saddle or harness.
Breeches Knee-length riding trousers (always worn with long boots).
Breed A group of horses or ponies that all look similar because they have been deliberately bred, over many generations, for certain characteristics.
Buck To leap in the air with arched back and all four feet off the ground.

Cannon bone Bone of the foreleg between knee and fetlock. It is also called the shin bone. On the hind leg this bone is called the shank.
Canter The pace between trot and gallop. It consists of three beats and a moment when all four legs are off the ground.
Cantle The rear part of the saddle seat.
Change of rein Change of direction in the arena. When circling to the left, the pony is said to be on the left rein.
Chaps Leather leggings worn over riding trousers. Half-chaps cover only the calves, between knee and ankle.
Cheek The part of the bit outside the mouth. It connects the mouthpiece of the bit to the bridle and to the reins.
Cheekpiece The part of the bridle that connects the headpiece to the bit.
Chestnut Horny growth on the inside of each of the horse's legs. (Chestnut is also a color description for a rich brown coat.)
Chukka Polo term for the 7½-minute periods into which the game is divided.
Clear round In a showjumping competition, the jumping of the whole course without knocking down any of the fences.
Coldblood Describes the native horses of Europe, especially the heavy draught types.
Collection One of the variations within a pace (e.g., collected trot, collected canter).

When collected, the pony's outline is shortened and rounded. The hindquarters are carried lower than the forehand so that most of the pony's weight is carried over the hind legs. The neck is raised and arched, and the nose is held in a vertical position. Collection is the opposite of extension.
Colt Uncastrated male horse or pony under four years old.
Conformation The shape of the animal; the skeletal and muscular proportions that together create the pony's overall appearance. A pony of good proportions, with straight, strong limbs and well-shaped neck, back and quarters is said to have good conformation.
Contact The contact between the pony and the rider through the reins and the rider's legs.
Crest The topline of the neck.
Croup The highest point of the hindquarters, between the tail and the loins.
Curb bit A bit with long cheeks and a chain that lies in the curb groove. It works as a lever and is usually worn along with a snaffle as part of a double bridle.
Curb groove The groove behind the jaw in which the chain of the curb bit lies.

Diagonal The diagonal is formed by the foreleg and its opposite hind leg moving and coming to the ground together. (This happens in trot.)
Dismount To get off a horse.
Dock The bony part of the tail on which the hair grows.
Double bridle A bridle that has two bits and two sets of reins. It is used to enable the advanced dressage rider to give very precise aids.

Engagement A horse or pony is said to be engaged when the hind legs are brought well under the body, enabling the pony to move with greater energy.
Entire An uncastrated male horse.
Ergot Horny growth on the back of the fetlock.
Exercise Riding for the purpose of maintaining a pony's fitness. Also the practising of particular moves in the arena in order to improve the rider's and pony's skills.
Extension Variation on a pace (e.g., extended trot). It is the opposite of collection in that the pony's stride and outline lengthens.

Farrier A person qualified to fit shoes on horses and to look after the general health of the foot.
Feathers Long hair on the lower legs and fetlocks. Feathers are usually associated with heavy horses and coldblood breeds.
Fetlock The joint that connects the foot and pastern to the cannon (or shank).
Filly A female horse or pony under four years old.
Flehmen The curling back of the lips. Stallions usually do this as a reaction to a mare in season, but many horses do it in response to unusual tastes or smells.
Foal Colt, gelding, or filly up to a year old.
Forearm Upper part of the foreleg above the knee.
Forehand The part of the pony's body in front of the girth. It includes the head, neck, shoulder, withers, and forelegs.
Forelock The section of mane that lies between the ears and falls over the forehead.
Frog The rubbery, V-shaped pad on the sole of the foot. The frog acts as a shock-absorber. When picking out the feet, the frog should be treated gently.

Gait Another word for pace. The four main gaits (or paces) are walk, trot, canter, and gallop. It can also mean a variation within a pace, such as collected canter, extended trot, and so on.
Gallop The fastest pace. It has four beats and a period of suspension – a moment when all four feet are off the ground.
Gaskin The section of the hind leg between the hock and the stifle. Also called the second thigh.
Gelding A castrated male horse.
Girth The circumference of the body measured behind the withers and around the barrel. It also describes the wide strap used to secure the saddle.
Grids A series of jumps set up to improve the horse's fitness and jumping technique. This type of training is called gridwork.
Gridwork See grids.
Gymkhana Originally gymnastic displays on horseback. Now used to describe various mounted games, including bending race, egg-and-spoon race, and so on.

Hack To ride outside the arena or school, for the simple purpose of exercise and pleasure rather than for schooling. (In showing, the word hack describes a type of elegant riding horse.).
Half-chaps See chaps.
Halter See headcollar.

Hand Unit of measurement used in measuring the horse from highest point of the wither to the ground. One hand equals 4 inches (10.2cm).

Headcollar A simple piece of headwear (consisting principally of a noseband and headpiece) to which a leadrope is attached for leading the pony or tying him up.

Headpiece The part of the bridle that rests behind the pony's ears. Below the level of the browband it splits into two: one section fastens to the cheekpieces; the other forms the throatlatch.

Hindquarters The part of the body behind the saddle: from the back of the flanks to the top of the tail down to the top of the gaskin. Often called simply the quarters.

Hock A joint of the hind leg, between the stifle and the fetlock.

Hotblood Term used to describe the Arab and Thoroughbred.

Indoor school Indoor arena

In front of the bit A pony is in front of the bit when he is pulling hard. In doing this he is ignoring the rider's instructions.

In-hand Describes a horse being led, such as when competing in "halter" classes.

Inside and outside Describes the side to which the pony is bending. So if you are riding a circle to the left, your inside rein (or leg, etc.) is the left one.

Jodhpurs Ankle-length trousers specially designed for riding.

Jump-off The final round in a show-jumping competition, in which riders that have completed clear rounds compete against the clock to decide the winner.

Leathers The straps bearing the stirrup irons. *See* stirrups.

Loins Area either side of the spine lying just behind the saddle.

Manège Arena used for schooling.

Mare Female horse or pony aged four years or over.

Martingale A piece of tack that joins the saddle to the reins (or bridle) in order to prevent the horse from throwing his head up.

Mount To get on a horse.

Near (side) Left (side).

Noseband The part of the bridle that surrounds the nose. There are various types, each having a slightly different action.

Numnah See saddle blanket.

Off (side) Right (side).

Outside and inside *See* inside and outside.

On the bit This describes a horse that is accepting the bit. The head is carried in a near-vertical position and the mouth is a little below the line of the rider's hand.

Paces The sequence of footfalls in movement. The four main paces are walk, trot, canter gallop. It can also mean a variation within a pace, such as collected canter, extended trot, and so on.

Poll The point between the pony's ears at which the head meets the neck.

Pastern The section of the leg between the foot and the fetlock.

Points The parts of the horse, e.g. stifle, hock, knee, dock, and so on. When used in relation to color it refers to lower legs, mane, and tail (e.g., bay with black points).

Pommel The front arch of the saddle.

Purebred Horse of a pure breed, i.e., with both parents of the same breed.

Quarters See hindquarters.

Rear To lift the forequarters and stand on the hind legs. Some ponies do this out of excitement, but others may do it in a deliberate attempt to unseat the rider.

Rising to the trot Describes the rider lifting the seat slightly out of the saddle on one beat of the trot and returning it to the saddle on the next beat. This is also sometimes called posting.

Saddle blanket A pad or cloth placed under the saddle.

Saddler A person who makes tack. A good saddler will also fit tack to ensure it is comfortable for your pony to wear.

School An arena in which to practise school movements.

Schooling Training.

Schooling whip A long whip (about 120cm/42in), used especially in dressage to reinforce the leg aids. Sometimes called a dressage whip.

School movements The exercises carried out in the arena. When figures of eight or serpentine shapes are ridden they are called "school figures."

Season The time during which a mare is capable of becoming pregnant. Mares come into season once a year.

Second thigh See gaskin.

Shank Hind cannon bone.

Sheath The protective fold of skin covering the male pony's penis.

Sitting trot In sitting trot, the rider keeps his or her seat in the saddle, rather than rising every other beat.

Snaffle mouth A pony is said to have a snaffle mouth if he can be ridden in a mild snaffle bridle in all circumstances. Such a pony does not need stronger bits for certain disciplines.

Sound A sound horse is one in good physical health with no bodily defects and with no faults in action.

Stallion An uncastrated male horse of four years old or more.

Stifle The next joint up from the hock on the hind leg. It is the pony's equivalent to the human knee.

Stirrup iron See stirrups

Stirrups Describes the irons (in which the rider's foot rests) as well as the leather strap by which the irons are attached to the saddle.

Stride A completed sequence of footfalls and leg movements within a pace. So one stride of walk consists of four footfalls (beats), while a canter stride consists of three footfalls plus a moment of suspension. The distances between showjumps are measured in strides (the distance a pony covers in one stride)

Suspension The point in a horse's pace at which all four feet are off the ground (as happens in canter).

Tack Saddlery, especially saddle and bridle.

Throatlatch The slim strap that passes from the headpiece of the bridle under the throat. It is fastened on the left side. (Pronouned *throatlash*.)

Topline The outline of the back from wither to croup.

Trot The pace between walk and canter. It has two beats in which the legs move in opposite diagonal pairs. See diagonal.

Turnout Dress and appearance of a horse or pony and his rider.

Type A horse of no particular breed but recognizable as belonging to a group used for a particular purpose, e.g., cob, hunter, polo pony.

Walk The first of the four main paces. It has four beats.

Warmblood A horse that has a percentage of Thoroughbred and/or Arab blood. Warmbloods are often specifically bred as sports horses, i.e., for showjumping, cross-country, and so on.

Whip One of the artificial aids. It should be used behind the rider's leg, or occasionally on the shoulder. Its purpose is to reinforce the rider's signals, in other words to back up your instructions if the pony is not listening to you. The good rider never uses it excessively and certainly never in anger. The whip used for general work is usually a jumping whip, which is shorter than a schooling whip.

Withers The bony point at the base of the neck, above the line of the shoulder.

Work Concentrated exercise, usually carried out in the arena.

Index

Acknowledgments

Author's Acknowledgments
Putting together and writing *Fun with Ponies and Horses* has been the greatest fun! The enjoyment that all those involved got out of taking part in its production proved the point and the purpose of the book—that having a pony should be fun.

Thank you to all our pony riders: Anna Bird, Milly Coleman-Straw, Hannah Cook, Victoria (Tori) Hoper, Matthew Hoper, Sophie Kurton, Hayley Lane, Shannon Lunt, Tom Macleod, James Ridley, Rachel Ridley, Phoebe Windsor-Clive, Laura Dudfield, Jenny Clemments, Eleanor Rudd, Kathryn Rudd, their parents, and their ponies for the patience and good humor shown throughout. Thank you to Sally Thomas and Jessica Garton for their help in controlling ponies and people; to Kit Houghton for his excellent photography; and to Studio Cactus for putting it all together.

Enjoying horses and ponies, as with many things in life, comes down to having confidence in yourself and in what you are doing. I hope this book will give those who read it the confidence to enjoy themselves fully. Personally, I am eternally grateful to the people in my life who have given me the confidence to do things the way I believe is right; my husband, Martin, my family and, in specific equestrian circles, Dot Willis and the late Baron Eric de Wykerslooth. I have only touched on the basics of their principles in this book but their training system and approach is what has given me the confidence and ability to do what I do.

Packager's Acknowledgments
Studio Cactus would like to thank Julia Cady for proofreading; Lynda Swindells for indexing; Susan McBane for Americanizing; Aaron Brown, Sue Gordon, and Abbey Cookson-Moore for editorial assistance.

Picture Credits
All photographs were taken by Kit Houghton or Studio Cactus.